ALBERT
Ellis

Key Figures in Counselling and Psychotherapy

Series editor: Windy Dryden

The *Key Figures in Counselling and Psychotherapy* series of books provides a concise, accessible introduction to the lives, contributions and influence of the leading innovators whose theoretical and practical work has had a profound impact on counselling and psychotherapy. The series includes comprehensive overviews of:

Sigmund Freud
by Michael Jacobs

Eric Berne
by Ian Stewart

Carl Rogers
by Brian Thorne

Melanie Klein
by Julia Segal

Fritz Perls
by Petrūska Clarkson and Jennifer Mackewn

Aaron T. Beck
by Marjorie E. Weishaar

ALBERT
Ellis

Joseph Yankura
Windy Dryden

SAGE Publications
London • Newbury Park • New Delhi

First published 1994

SAGE Publications Ltd
6 Bonhill Street
London EC2A 4PU

SAGE Publications Inc
2455 Teller Road
Thousand Oaks, California 91320

SAGE Publications India Pvt Ltd
32, M-Block Market
Greater Kailash – I
New Delhi 110 048

British Library Cataloguing in Publication data

A catalogue record for this book is available from the British
Library.

ISBN 0 8039 8528 2
ISBN 0 8039 8529 0 pbk

Library of Congress catalog card number 94-67489

Typeset by Mayhew Typesetting, Rhayader, Powys
Printed in Great Britain by Biddles Ltd, Guildford

Contents

Preface

We are pleased to add this volume on Albert Ellis, the creator of rational emotive behaviour therapy (REBT), to the Sage series entitled Key Figures in Counselling and Psychotherapy. Ellis's pioneering clinical work greatly influenced the development of the cognitive-behavioural revolution in psychotherapy, and has stimulated and inspired countless therapy trainees and practitioners. Ellis has invented and promoted an approach to the treatment of emotional disturbance that is effective, efficient and comparatively easy to teach to therapists-in-training. This book will provide the reader with an overview of his ideas on the theory and practice of REBT, as well as a review of some of the major criticisms to which his work has been subjected.

Despite his voluminous writings and his seemingly tireless efforts to publicly present his views on psychotherapy to lay and professional audiences, Ellis has often been misunderstood and misrepresented. Some laypersons and mental health professionals regard him as an opportunistic publicity-seeker who has made himself wealthy through his numerous self-help books and public appearances. While Ellis certainly could live in an opulent manner on the royalties earned by some of his books, he indulges in few luxuries and lives an almost Spartan lifestyle. He turns over the income from his lectures, clinical practice, and book royalties to the non-profit Institute for Rational-Emotive Therapy in New York City. The Institute, which has been located at its present site since 1964, provides professional training in REBT, offers workshops and lectures on REBT to the general public, and operates a moderately priced clinic where clients can receive both individual and group therapy.

If Ellis has acted as a publicity-seeker, there is little in his history to suggest that he has been motivated by the prospect of material gain. Rather, his efforts to maintain a high profile within the mental health field have been largely propelled by his strong desire to promote an approach to therapy which, in his view, holds potential benefits for a great many human beings. Ellis's basic message in this regard is quite clear: accept primary responsibility for your emotional problems and work in a determined fashion to combat the irrational thinking which underpins them, and you can minimize your self-defeating upsets and enhance your chances for happiness and satisfaction. Many thousands of REBT clients and workshop participants have heard and applied this message, and have been significantly helped by it.

Ever the passionate sceptic, Ellis has repeatedly assailed the edifice of established orthodoxy over the course of his long professional career. Thus, he has been a critic of psychoanalysis (as well as a number of other widely practised therapies), restrictive sexual mores, environmental theories of emotional disturbance, religiosity, certain behaviour therapy techniques and Alcoholics Anonymous. He, in turn, has become an object of criticism. As the reader will see in Chapter 4, Ellis's theory and therapy have drawn much critical scrutiny. Ellis has responded to much of this criticism and has used it as an opportunity to clarify and further develop his ideas.

We have made liberal use of excerpts from Ellis's writings throughout this book. It is our hope that these excerpts will make for a livelier text (Ellis's writing style can be both provocative and evocative), as well as provide the reader with a better feel for the person and his ideas.

A note about some of the terminology employed in this work. In 1993, Ellis changed the name of his approach from 'rational-emotive therapy' (RET) to 'rational emotive *behaviour* therapy' (REBT). He did this in order to emphasize its behavioural components. Thus, in order to be up to date, we make reference throughout the text to 'rational emotive behaviour therapy' and 'REBT'. However, when reproducing excerpts from writings published prior to Ellis's 1993 name change, we have retained the terms 'rational-emotive therapy' and 'RET'. Also, we have used the term 'rational-emotive' as an adjective to describe nouns such as 'theory' and 'philosophy'. We felt that a phrase such as 'rational emotive behavioural philosophy' would simply be an unnecessary annoyance for readers to have to encounter time and again within the text.

We hope that this book provides a useful introduction to Albert Ellis and rational emotive behaviour therapy. We would, however, encourage interested readers to engage in further research to broaden and deepen their understanding of the REBT approach to treating client problems. To this end, we have provided a select bibliography that follows the book's final chapter.

Joseph Yankura　　　　　　　　　　　　　　*Windy Dryden*
New York　　　　　　　　　　　　　　　　　*London*

1

The Life of Albert Ellis

I do not believe that the events of my childhood greatly influenced my becoming a psychotherapist, nor oriented me to becoming the kind of individual and the type of therapist that I now am. That notion is the 'psychoanalytic bag', and fortunately I am no longer suffocating in that particular bag.

(Ellis, 1991a: 1)

Family Background

Albert Ellis was born on 27 September 1913, in Pittsburgh, Pennsylvania. He was the first of three children born to Hettie and Henry Ellis. He had a brother, Paul, who was one and a half years younger than himself, and a sister, Janet, who was four years younger. Ellis's brother and sister are both now deceased.

When young Albert was 4, his family moved to New York City, perhaps because his father was in search of better business prospects. Ellis has lived in New York City since that time.

Childhood Years: Three Challenges

As the quote at the start of this chapter indicates, Albert Ellis discounts the notion that the events of his childhood had much to do with shaping the sort of person (and psychotherapist) he eventually grew into. In his view, his innate tendencies to be an active problem-solver and to make the best of adverse circumstances were much more important determinants of the path his life would take.

This has been his view of himself throughout his professional life; it is clearly in congruence with the view of human beings he espouses within his rational-emotive theories of psychotherapy and personality. Back in the late 1950s and early 1960s, when behaviourists were emphasizing the role of the environment in determining an individual's adjustment or maladjustment, Ellis was advancing and developing arguments in support of his hypotheses concerning the biological basis of human irrationality (Ellis, 1976a, 1979a). His positions on this issue were unique for their time, considering that they were at variance with the prevailing *zeitgeist*. Contemporary developmental psychology, with its emphasis on the relationship between inborn temperament and personality, might perhaps be considered as offering some degree of validation of Ellis's theories in this regard.

Nevertheless, it is possible to identify circumstances and events in Ellis's childhood that most biographers would regard as significant (or at the very least, interesting). Even if, as Ellis maintains, these circumstances and events did not largely shape his personality nor determine his life's course, they can be viewed as challenges which encouraged the expression of the innate tendencies referred to above. This section will outline three major challenges which confronted Ellis as a child, and will then describe the manner in which he responded to them. Hopefully, Ellis's responses to these challenges will provide the reader with some insights concerning his personality.

Challenge One: 'Benign' Parental Neglect

The first challenge relates to the circumstances of Ellis's home life, and the sort of parenting he received. Ellis's father was a travelling salesman and promoter, and was often away from home for extended periods of time. When he *was* at home, he was usually so involved with his own business and leisure interests that, as Ellis describes it, 'my younger brother and sister and I literally spent about five minutes a day with him, kissing him goodbye in the morning, just before we scooted off to school' (Ellis, 1991a: 2). Albert's parents divorced when he was 12 years old; after that his father was rarely around and provided little financial support for the family.

Ellis's mother may have been *physically* present in the home on a more frequent basis, but was apparently quite disinterested in housekeeping or caring for her children. Ellis has described her thus:

> As for my nice Jewish mother, a hell of a lot of help she was! Born at least 20 years before her time, thrown out of school in the sixth grade for compulsive talking, and quite unequipped to deal adequately with either marriage or child-rearing, she was much more immersed in her own pleasures and her own ego-aggrandizing activities than she was in understanding and taking care of her children. Her typical day: she arose about eight forty-five . . . She sloppily and desultorily did a minimum of cleaning, shopping and child-tending. She spent most afternoons at her Temple sisterhood functions or playing bridge or mah-jongg with some

of her women friends. She returned home around five or six . . . She cooked or brought home from the delicatessen very simple, ill-prepared meals that required a minimum of effort. And she spent most nights with her friends (most of them 15 or more years younger than she and from a lower socioeconomic stratum), quite unrelated to her children (and often out of the house, leaving them unattended, in the charge of son Albert). (1991a: 2)

Thus, Albert and siblings were exposed to a degree of parental neglect that, in this day and age, might have prompted a phone call to Child Protective Services by some concerned school teacher or neighbour. The family apparently never had any involvement with any social welfare agency, however, and the Ellis children were left to cope as best they could. Young Albert's response to this sort of home environment, to be described below, reveals his general approach to dealing with adverse life circumstances.

Challenge Two: Poor Health in Childhood

The second major challenge faced by Ellis as a child is related to a series of health problems he experienced. When he was 5 years old, he had tonsilitis which developed into a serious strep infection. Emergency surgery was required to save his life; subsequent to this surgery, he developed acute nephritis (Wiener, 1988). He was hospitalized eight or so times between the ages of 5 and 7, mainly because of the nephritis; one of these hospitalizations was for a period of approximately ten months. As one might predict after reading about the parental neglect described above, Albert was less frequently visited by his mother during his hospital stays than were other children in the hospital and his father rarely visited. In fact, days and sometimes weeks would pass without his receiving a family visit (Wiener, 1988). During convalescent periods at home, he was restricted from engaging in the usual physical games and sports of childhood.

Challenge Three: Shyness and Social Avoidance

Ellis describes himself as having been unusually shy and introverted as a child, and the task of dealing with his shyness can be regarded as the third significant challenge he faced in his childhood (and later, his adolescence). In school he steered clear of public performances as much as possible, and would not participate in events such as classroom plays. He also avoided making social overtures to most of the neighbourhood girls and female classmates upon whom he developed crushes. He was not always successful in his attempts to navigate around the sorts of situations that were anxiety-provoking for him: 'I sometimes had to recite a poem in class or ascend the auditorium podium to accept an award, and at these times I sweated and sizzled with anxiety and desperately looked for (and sometimes managed to cleverly find) some way out' (Ellis, 1991a: 3).

Dealing with Childhood Challenges

How did Ellis cope with these three significant challenges of his childhood? By his own account, the parental neglect he endured did not impact upon him in any seriously adverse fashion. In fact, he appears to have thrived on the extra independence and autonomy it afforded him. He has stated, 'I decided not to hate my mother for her ineptness and used it instead to twist her around my little finger, and even in some ways to exploit her' (Ellis, 1991a: 3). He governed his own behaviour so that he was able to garner attention and rewards from the adults in his interpersonal environment (in contrast to his brother Paul, who was always getting himself into trouble), and became skilful in taking care of himself and his two younger siblings. He would, for example, get himself up in the morning with his own alarm clock, prepare breakfast for himself and then walk to school on his own (which meant crossing several very busy city thoroughfares). He greatly enjoyed his early school experience (with the exception of the previously mentioned public performance situations), and achieved an excellent academic record. Reportedly, he sometimes regretted that school wasn't open on weekends (Wiener, 1988).

With respect to his illnesses and frequent hospitalizations, the child Albert Ellis again displayed a rather remarkable degree of adaptability and a determination to make the best of unfortunate circumstances. He reportedly became a leader among the children on the hospital ward during one of his lengthy visits, and quite likely lost a bit of his shyness in the process (Wiener, 1988). If he often felt miserable and pined for his family during his hospital stays, he has never acknowledged it in any of the published accounts of his life.

Perhaps partly as a result of the physical restrictions placed upon him during his convalescent periods, Ellis developed a concern for his health and seems to have never developed an affinity for the rough-and-tumble games that can characterize the boyhood years. Instead, he became increasingly drawn toward more intellectual pursuits and interests. His choice of reading material quickly became more sophisticated than that of his young contemporaries, and by age 8 or so he had read through every volume of an encyclopaedia (the *Book of Knowledge*) that his family had acquired.

Ellis was less successful in dealing with his self-described shyness during his childhood years, insofar as he failed to overcome it completely. As he describes it, he 'protected' his shyness (meaning that he allowed it to continue) by assiduously avoiding the sorts of social situations that were problematic for him. However, despite his deficits in athletic ability (at least in comparison with his brother, Paul), his fear of public presentations, and his anxiety about approaching girls, he was able to avoid feelings of low self-worth. According to his account (Ellis, 1991a), this was mainly because he based his self-esteem upon his intelligence, his school achievements and the favourable social responses he received from friends and adults. Thus, although his shyness continued to plague him until early adulthood, he was seemingly able to structure his world so that it didn't cause him too much trouble.

It is important to note that when he reflects upon his childhood years, Ellis acknowledges that 'I basically liked myself for the wrong reasons' (1991a: 4). He is referring here to the fact that he based his sense of self-worth upon his achievements, which runs counter to REBT's non-person-rating philosophy. According to the REBT position on self-esteem issues (to be treated more fully in Chapter 2), it is more psychologically healthy for individuals to replace their self-rating tendencies with a philosophy of unconditional self-acceptance.

In Ellis's view, the difficult circumstances of his childhood helped to hone his innate capacity to be a determined and effective problem-solver. Rather than allowing himself to succumb to emotional misery, he applied his considerable intellectual endowment to the task of finding ways to make the best of adverse circumstances. He was able to adapt to the neglect of his parents, successfully compensate for the constraints placed upon him by poor health, and minimize the impact of his social-evaluative anxiety.

Ellis does not believe that the challenges he faced as a child *caused* him to become a more rational human being. In support of this position he cites the case of his sister, who was exposed to childhood circumstances just as difficult as his own. She was apparently a chronically unhappy youngster, who grew into an adult with some significant emotional problems. Ellis attributes this to the fact that 'she was partly born with a whiny, demanding, injustice-collecting temperament' such that 'she *chose* to make the worst of her childhood conditions' (1991a: 4).

As will be seen in subsequent chapters, an emphasis upon the importance of innate temperament carries important implications for a theory of psychotherapy. In Ellis's formulation of REBT, individuals are viewed as being born with varying capacities for rational thinking; those who are more prone to think irrationally or self-defeatingly will very likely experience more frequent episodes of significant emotional disturbance. Even with a strong tendency toward irrational thinking, however, individuals can, with concerted effort, make themselves less vulnerable to self-defeating emotions and behaviours.

Ellis left his childhood years and entered adolescence with his shyness largely intact. The section that follows will detail the manner in which he directed his own efforts and energies to finally conquer this emotional handicap. In addition, it will describe the circumstances that led to his decision to pursue a career in the field of mental health.

Adolescence and Early Adulthood

As noted earlier, Ellis began to display intellectual tendencies as a child, partly as a result of his prolonged periods of illness and recuperation. By the age of 13 he was reading H.G. Wells and Upton Sinclair; at 16 he had discovered the writings of Epictetus (an ancient Stoic philosopher), Spinoza, Kant and Bertrand Russell. Ellis attended the New York High School of Commerce, an all-male school, during his adolescence, and graduated at 16. Although he applied himself very little to studying, he was ranked seventh in a class of approximately 150 students.

At the age of 12, Ellis decided that he wanted to become a writer. He hoped, in fact, to become a renowned novelist. Realizing, however, that he would have to develop some means of supporting himself until he achieved success as a writer, he decided to enter (along with his brother, Paul, and boyhood friend, Manny Birnbaum) the Baruch School of Business and Civic Administration of the City College of New York when he was about to be 17 years old. His plan was to become trained as an accountant, quickly make enough money in business to live off, and then pursue his writing projects.

Unfortunately, Ellis's plan to quickly become rich through business was foiled by the Great Depression. Good jobs and business opportunities were quite scarce during this period, and Ellis had to work at a number of relatively low-level jobs in order to make ends meet.

Meanwhile, in his early 20s, Ellis finally managed to overcome his public speaking phobia and his fear of approaching and speaking to girls. He attributes his success in this arena to insights he gained through his readings in practical philosophy and to his application of *in vivo* desensitization techniques. He learned about the latter by reading about American behaviourist John B. Watson's experiments in conditioning and deconditioning fear responses in young children (Watson and Rayner, 1920). In his own words, Ellis worked on and conquered his anxiety about speaking with women in the following way:

Take . . . the matter of my early shyness . . . being terribly afraid of making contact with new girls until I was in my early twenties, and maneuvering my male friends into making the initial contacts . . . I realized that I was maintaining and even exacerbating my anxieties by that kind of evasive behavior.

I therefore laboriously taught myself, first, to challenge my anxiety-creating philosophies – namely, my beliefs that it would be awful if I got rejected, that I absolutely must not fail in making sexual–social overtures, and that if I did fail I was indubitably a lousy person who was therefore doomed to fail forever in this kind of somewhat risky pursuit. I kept fighting these internalized and long-held beliefs until I truly started to believe that no matter how many times I might fail or how foolish I might look to others while failing, I was still only a person who failed rather than a Failure with a capital F.

That was, theoretically, all well and good. But what really cured me of my shyness in this regard was thinking plus action. For before I could get rid of my fear of being rejected in making overtures to girls, I had to force myself, scores of times, to approach strange females, to make friendly overtures to them, to get rejected on many occasions, and to convince myself that the world did not come to an end, that I was not a shit, and that it merely was too damned bad that I wasn't getting accepted as I would like to be. After enough of this deliberate practice at risk-taking, I got to be one of the most accomplished woman-chasers and overture-makers in the Bronx Botanical Gardens (one of my main hangouts during my young days) and (later) the world at large. (Ellis, 1972a: 113–14)

Currently, when giving lectures or workshops to both professional and lay audiences, Ellis will sometimes cite his early 'risk-taking exercises' in the Bronx Botanical Gardens as an experience that influenced his eventual formulation of the principles and techniques of REBT. When he tells this tale to an audience, he relates that he set himself the task of starting conversations with and making social overtures to a hundred individual women within one month, in his nineteenth year, when he was on vacation from college. By his report, of the women he approached, only one assented to go out with him – and she subsequently failed to show up for the date!

To Ellis, this experience highlights several important features of human change processes in psychotherapy. First, in his view, it illustrates the fact that individuals who wish to change long standing patterns of self-defeating emotions and behaviours will probably have to push themselves repeatedly into situations and activities that will initially feel uncomfortable (that is, anxiety provoking) and unnatural. Secondly it serves to highlight the desirability of both thinking *and* acting against self-defeating emotions and behaviours. Thirdly, it underscores the efficiency and effectiveness of employing a flooding approach (as opposed to gradual desensitization) in the service of overcoming fears and inhibitions. Finally, as Ellis sees it, it demonstrates that external reinforcement for engaging in new, alternative behaviours is not a necessary condition for meaningful change to occur. Ellis certainly did not receive much reinforcement for his social risk-taking exercises with young women, yet he persisted in his efforts because of his strong desire to become free from anxiety and out of his conviction that he could (with repeated effort) overcome his problem in this regard.

As a young adult, Ellis was more successful in overcoming his shyness than he was at becoming a published writer. His lack of success in being published, however, was not due to a lack of effort on his part. While still in college, he produced a 500,000-word autobiographical novel. Between the ages of 19 and 28 he had completed approximately twenty full-length manuscripts, including several novels, plays and books of poems. None of these manuscripts were accepted for publication. He also produced a number of non-fiction works on sex, philosophy and politics (stemming from an emerging desire to influence and enlighten a mass audience in these areas), including a socialist primer based on *Das Kapital* that presented (and debunked) Marx's theory of surplus value in a simple question-and-answer format. While this volume came close to being accepted for publication, it too ultimately never found its way to press.

During this period of his life, Ellis describes himself as having been a 'liberal-democratic radical' (Ellis, 1972a). He subscribed to a number of views and beliefs that were quite revolutionary (given the sociocultural tenor of the time), and recognized that certain other writers with revolutionary views were having some success in having their ideas conveyed in print. Realizing at this point that he was probably not going to become the Great American Novelist, he determined 'to devote a good part of my life to promulgating the sex–family revolution, which most of my fellow radicals were sadly neglecting' (Ellis, 1972a: 110).

In this vein, he began to assemble a huge amount of material for an ambitious book which he titled, *The Case for Sexual Promiscuity*. He completed the manuscript and sent it around to various publishing houses, but again received nothing but rejection letters in return. Nearly twenty years later, in 1965, part of this work was published under the somewhat less provocative title, *The Case for Sexual Liberty* (Ellis, 1965a). During the intervening years, however, Ellis had already gained fame (and notoriety) as an authority and author in the sex/love area.

In order to produce his original manuscript for *The Case for Sexual Promiscuity*, Ellis conducted extensive research in the fields of sex, love and marriage. He read voluminously, and took copious notes on his readings. Friends soon learned of the research he was doing, and began to regard him as somewhat of an expert on sex and love issues. Some of these friends would come to him for consultation on their own particular sex and love problems. Despite the fact that Ellis regarded himself at that time as being less sexually experienced than most of these individuals, he has claimed that he was able to help them considerably with the information and advice he provided. In addition, he discovered that he greatly enjoyed doing this sort of 'counselling' work. At this point of his life, at about 28 years of age, he made a fateful choice that would eventually have a significant impact on the fields of counselling and psychotherapy:

> Since my writing was still getting me nowhere financially, and since I had done very well in several business jobs over the years but had no real liking for commercial ventures, I decided that it was time to get a real profession and some status as a counselor – so I began graduate training in psychology. (Ellis, 1991a: 7)

Graduate School Years

Ellis applied for admission to Columbia University in New York City, believing it to have the best graduate psychology department at that time. He was almost refused admission, however, because the programme of study he had completed at City College included almost no science courses. Thus, despite his far-ranging reading in such areas as biology, sociology, astronomy, political science and psychology, he was deemed to have an inadequate background in the sciences. Fortunately, he was able to strike a deal with the head of Columbia's psychology programme (Henry Garrett) wherein he proposed that if he took two graduate courses in psychology during the summer term and did well in them, he would be permitted to matriculate. He subsequently received A's in both classes, and began full-time graduate studies at Columbia in 1941.

Soon after starting at Columbia, Ellis realized that his department was not very supportive of clinical psychology or his interests in the areas of sex, family and marital therapy. He therefore entered the rival clinical psychology programme at Teachers College of Columbia University (then known as the Psychological Services Department) in September 1942. Ellis gained his master's degree in one year, and continued on towards the Doctor of Philosophy degree. He encountered no difficulties in completing his course work, but ran into serious problems while working on his doctoral dissertation.

In line with his interests in the areas of sex, love and marriage (and following his introduction to Alfred C. Kinsey's landmark research on sexual behaviour), Ellis chose to do his doctoral research on the love emotions of college women. He had passed his dissertation seminars and collected all of the data for this project (by way of a questionnaire he had designed), when any further progress was blocked by his department. Apparently, some of the faculty at Teachers College feared that Ellis's 'sex research' would generate negative publicity for the university. Ellis was eventually able to persuade most of the professors in his department that his hypotheses, methods and tentative conclusions were all quite legitimate, but he found that two senior faculty members were immovably opposed to his work. Anticipating that they would attempt to sabotage him and keep him from completing his degree, Ellis sadly abandoned his work on love in favour of a much less controversial topic. He quickly completed a dissertation on *A Comparison of the Use of Direct and Indirect Phrasing with Personality Questionnaires* (Ellis, 1947a), received his degree, and thereby finished his formal training at Teachers College. His thorough review of the literature on paper-and-pencil personality tests made him something of an acknowledged expert in this area, and a number of his earliest professional journal publications dealt with this subject (Ellis, 1946, 1947a, b, 1948a, b). He ultimately found research and writing on personality tests to be relatively boring, and became refocused on his main interests of sex, love and psychotherapy.

Early Career and Professional Development

Ellis began a small private practice in psychotherapy in 1943, soon after he received his master's degree in clinical psychology. His first regular job subsequent to receiving his PhD was as senior clinical psychologist at the Northern New Jersey Mental Hygiene Clinic. Ellis had already published a number of articles and reviews in the areas of sex and personality tests, and prepared twelve additional research papers during his first year in his new position. State psychologists and psychiatrists apparently produced little publishable research at that time, and Ellis's publications won him favour with administrators in the New Jersey State Department of Institutions and Agencies. As a result, when the new State Diagnostic Center opened its doors for the first time in 1949, Ellis was appointed its chief psychologist. He gained a great deal of clinical experience and honed his diagnostic skills to a considerable degree during the period he spent at these two placements.

In 1950 Ellis was made chief psychologist of the entire Department of Institutions and Agencies. He attributes his rapid rise within the state system primarily to his outstanding publishing record (Ellis, 1991a). By the end of 1950 he had published a total of forty-six articles and reviews and also had a book (*The Folklore of Sex*) in press (Ellis, 1951).

During the 1940s, psychoanalysis was still the pre-eminent and most widely respected form of psychotherapy in practice. Therefore, in order to increase his skills (and respectability) as a therapist, Ellis sought psychoanalytic training shortly after he received his doctoral degree. Although there were no legitimate analytic training institutes at that time that would accept non-physicians as trainees, Ellis managed to arrange a training analysis with Dr Charles Hulbeck (who had himself been analysed by Hermann Rorschach) of the Karen Horney Institute for Psychoanalysis. He spent six years (between 1947 and 1953) in analysis, with Hulbeck, and received psychoanalytic supervision on his own cases from him. After his first session with Hulbeck, during which he had free-associated almost non-stop for the entire hour, the analyst reportedly noted, 'My, you certainly can talk, can't you!' (Wiener, 1988).

Ellis used his psychoanalysis to help himself consider whether or not to marry his 'utterly charming and brilliant but abysmally *meshugge*' girlfriend of that time (Ellis, 1972a). He ultimately decided not to do so. In addition, Ellis has reported that he largely overcame his time neurosis during the period that he was in analysis (Ellis, 1972a; Wiener, 1988). He had been a compulsive worker and clock-watcher, and subscribed to the belief that he *had to* achieve all of his goals in order to be a worthwhile person. As a consequence of holding this belief, he was often rushing to get things done and frequently worried about the many tasks he had yet to complete. He came to realize, however, that his time on earth was limited and that he would probably not be able to accomplish everything he hoped for; he was also better able to accept his own limitations without engaging in negative self-evaluation. Although Ellis (1972a) has indicated that he is unsure how much of a role his analysis played in bringing about these positive changes, he has noted that they may have partly been due to the rather unconventional amalgam of Freudian–Horneyian interpretations, existential philosophy and common sense he received from his analyst.

Ellis's own analytic practice was doing well by the early 1950s. He greatly enjoyed the 'detectiving' work he did with his analysands (in terms of making connections between their childhood experiences and present-day problems), and believes that the results he got were as good as those attained by other analysts. He found, however, that a good number of his patients were unable to afford to have sessions with the frequency dictated by classical psychoanalysis. As a result, he would see some of these individuals only once a week, or once every other week. He abandoned his attempts to use classical analysis with such cases, and began to practise psychoanalytically oriented psychotherapy.

To his surprise, Ellis found that most of the patients exposed to this supposedly more 'superficial' approach fared as well or better than the patients who received classical analysis. In addition, he discovered that combining more direct methods (such as advice and information giving) with the relatively passive analytic procedures resulted in swifter and more complete improvements for patients.

Ellis was discovering on a first-hand basis that an active-directive approach to psychotherapy could be both more efficient and effective than the standard psychoanalytic approach.

Ellis started to become critical of the anti-scientific and passive aspects of the psychoanalytic approach to therapy, and authored several papers aimed at reforming the psychoanalytic movement from within (Ellis, 1949, 1950, 1956). Concurrently, he began formulating some of the theoretical principles and techniques of what he would call 'rational therapy'. In the mid-1950s, he published two papers which described the results of his experimentation with methods that deviated from psychoanalytic orthodoxy: 'New approaches to psychotherapy techniques' (Ellis, 1955a) and 'Psychotherapy techniques for use with psychotics' (Ellis, 1955b). Also, at about this time, Ellis began discussing his developing views on therapy with a small group of fellow mental health practitioners who would meet at his apartment. As his ideas concerning the practice of effective and efficient therapy took form, he became increasingly disenchanted with psychoanalysis. By 1953 he had almost completely rejected the psychoanalytic approach, and began to call himself a 'psychotherapist' rather than a 'psychoanalyst'. Ellis gave his first presentation on rational therapy to a professional audience at the American Psychological Association's annual convention in 1956, and published his first article about it ('Rational psychotherapy and individual psychology') in 1957.

Ellis left his post with the New Jersey mental health establishment in 1952, following a falling out with Sanford Bates, the Commissioner of the Department of Institutions and Agencies. According to Ellis's (1991a) account, Bates was shocked by the 'sexual liberalism' expressed in his recently published book, *The Folklore of Sex* (Ellis, 1951). In addition, Ellis had another book in progress at the time – *The Psychology of Sex Offenders* (Ellis and Brancale, 1956) – and Bates reportedly insisted that Dr Ralph Brancale (a psychiatrist and the director of the New Jersey State Diagnostic Center) be credited as the first author of this volume. Ellis resisted this pressure, as he had put far more work into the book than had his co-author. In August 1951, he was charged by Bates with illegitimately serving as chief psychologist for the state system because he was actually living in New York instead of New Jersey, and with inappropriately maintaining a private practice while working for the state.

Ellis viewed these charges as stemming from the enmity that Sanford Bates had for him, and saw them as being largely illegitimate. While it was true that government employees of the state of New Jersey were not permitted to live outside of the state, many of them (including some high-ranking officials) resided in the adjoining states of Pennsylvania and New York. In addition, while the state regulations of that time barred state *psychiatrists* (and other state physicians) from maintaining private practices, they did not prohibit psychologists from doing so. Ellis considered fighting the charges and his threatened dismissal from the New Jersey state system, but ultimately decided that he would not. He anticipated that even if he won his case, he would probably be blocked by Bates and his allies from implementing any of the improvements he had envisioned for the state mental health system. Ellis negotiated with Bates and agreed to leave his position on amicable terms (Ellis, 1991a). Subsequently he was able to devote even more time to his private practice, his writing and the development of his ideas concerning psychotherapy.

Early Development of Rational Emotive Behaviour Therapy

As noted earlier, Ellis gave his first professional presentation and published his first article on REBT in the second half of the 1950s. The popularity of this new therapeutic approach grew slowly at first, largely because Ellis was its sole public exponent. In this role, he encountered some stiff opposition from leading psychoanalysts, client-centred therapists and experiential therapists.

Ellis at first called his new approach, 'rational therapy', because he wanted to underscore the connection between rational thinking and psychological adjustment. Soon, however, he was inaccurately accused of being a proponent of eighteenth-century rationalism (a philosophical position that emphasizes the importance of reason and intellect above all other aspects of human experience), and of ignoring the role played by emotion in human functioning and psychological problems. This misunderstanding of Ellis's approach was perhaps not surprising, as he strongly emphasized the role of thinking in both the creation and remediation of emotional disturbance. In order to counter this misunderstanding, he changed the name of his approach to rational-emotive therapy. He changed it again in 1993, to rational emotive behaviour therapy, to underscore his use of behavioural techniques and activity homework assignments within treatment.

Professional and lay interest in rational emotive behaviour therapy grew in the late 1950s, as Ellis continued to write and lecture on it. In 1957 he published *How to Live with a Neurotic* (Ellis, 1957b), the first of his many rational-emotive self-help books. This was followed in 1958 by his book *Sex without Guilt*, which applied rational-emotive principles to sex problems and sex therapy. In 1959 Ellis founded a non-profit educational organization, the Institute for Rational Living, later to become the Institute for Rational-Emotive Therapy, which is still its official name at the time of writing. At the Institute he began to use REBT in group as well as individual therapy (Ellis, 1989a).

The Institute was located in Ellis's apartment in the Parc Vendôme building in New York City until 1965. Shortly after it was established, it began to sponsor public presentations and to offer training for therapists in REBT. In 1964, the Institute purchased a large New York town-house (located at 45 East 65th Street in Manhattan) with some of the royalties from Ellis's 1960 book, *The Art and Science of Love*. It has been housed in this building ever since.

In 1962, Ellis revised and published most of his early articles on REBT in book form in *Reason and Emotion in Psychotherapy*. This book represented his first attempt to present his ideas on therapy in a systematic and comprehensive form, and can be considered an early classic with respect to modern cognitive-behavioural therapy. *Reason and Emotion in Psychotherapy* presented the origins and essential elements of REBT, compared this approach to other popular therapeutic approaches, and attempted to respond to some of the objections that had been made to it by adherents to alternative schools of therapy. Ellis (1989a) credits this book with garnering significant professional support for his work.

The Mid-1960s and 1970s

Ellis continued to spread REBT's influence through his writings and presentations for both professional and lay audiences. Of note, in 1965 he began regularly offering a Friday evening workshop for the general public entitled 'Problems of Daily Living'. During this workshop, he provides live demonstrations of REBT with volunteer 'clients' from the audience. Following such a demonstration, audience members are given the opportunity to comment upon or ask questions about Ellis's therapeutic approach or the 'client's' problem area (for a detailed description of these workshops, see Dryden and Backx, 1987).

In the 1960s, the Institute for Rational-Emotive Therapy became chartered by the Regents of the State of New York, and began offering fellowship and associate fellowship training programmes. The Institute launched a journal, *Rational Living*, in 1967; this publication has expanded its scope over the years and is now known as the *Journal of Rational-Emotive and Cognitive-Behavior Therapy*.

The general field of cognitive-behavioural therapy gained particular prominence and respectability among mental health practitioners in the United States during the 1970s. Scores of studies concerned with treatment outcome and verification of theoretical tenets began to appear in the professional literature, and a number of influential books on REBT and cognitive-behavioural therapy found their way into print. These included works by Bandura (1977), Beck (1976; Beck, Rush, Shaw and Emery, 1979), Ellis (1971, 1973a; Ellis and Whiteley, 1979), Kendall and Hollon (1979), Lange and Jakubowski (1976), A.A. Lazarus (1971, 1976), Mahoney (1974), Meichenbaum (1977), Raimy (1975) and Spivack and Shure (1974). In addition, several popular self-help books employing the principles of REBT and cognitive-behavioural therapy appeared in bookstores: *Your Erroneous Zones* (Dyer, 1976), *Sex and the Liberated Man* (Ellis, 1976b), *A New Guide to Rational Living* (Ellis and Harper, 1975), and *I Can If I Want To* (Lazarus and Fay, 1975).

In the late 1960s, Ellis expanded REBT's application to include rational-emotive encounter marathon groups (Ellis, 1969). His marathons employed REBT's standard cognitive-behavioural procedures, and also included numerous experiential and emotive exercises and techniques. Originally, these marathon sessions lasted twenty-four hours or more. Ellis found, however, that such lengthy marathons were not justified by the results they achieved for participants. Ever concerned with efficiency in psychotherapy, he thus decided to shorten them to fourteen hours.

In the early 1970s the Institute established 'The Living School', which served children between the ages of 6 and 14. The Living School represented a significant experiment in preventative psychotherapy, as it attempted to provide students with an educational curriculum that included and incorporated the principles of REBT. It was hoped that students would learn (and internalize) the tenets of rational thinking, so that they would be less vulnerable to emotional disturbance as they proceeded through life. Unfortunately, the School terminated its programme after five years, and was unable to conduct any systematic outcome studies. It was difficult to define outcome criteria for such studies adequately, and follow-up on individual students proved problematic because families would move out of the area or transfer their children to schools with more extensive resources (for example, gym facilities). In addition, the Institute experienced some difficulty in retaining teachers for an extended period of time. Teachers left, for instance, in search of better-paying positions in public education. Despite its relatively short life, however, the Living School was judged a success by its directors, and parents of students expressed satisfaction with its programme (Wiener, 1988). In retrospect, it is rather remarkable that a moderately sized organization like the Institute was at all willing and able to sponsor such an ambitious project.

The 1970s also saw the debut of Ellis's rational humorous songs in front of a professional audience. These songs (to be described more fully in Chapter 3) combine humorous lyrics containing a rational message with a popular tune. Ellis sang some of his songs at the American Psychological Association's 1976 annual meeting during presentation of his paper, 'Fun as psychotherapy' (Ellis, 1977a). According to his version of events, this made him the hit of the convention! Ellis believes that when utilized by clients, these songs can represent a useful supplement to REBT's other self-help techniques.

The 1980s

At the start of the 1980s, Ellis's work was having a quite profound impact upon the fields of psychotherapy and counselling in the United States. According to an article by Smith (1982), a sample of 800 American clinical and counselling psychologists rated Ellis as second among the ten most influential psychotherapists (Carl Rogers received the first-place rating; Sigmund Freud came third). Heesacker, Heppner and Rogers (1982) analysed approximately 14,000 references cited in three major counselling psychology journals published in the United States and found that Ellis was the most frequently cited author after 1957. In 1985, Ellis received the American Psychological Association's Award for Distinguished Professional Contributions to Knowledge.[1] The citation for this award, published in the April 1986 edition of the professional journal *American Psychologist* (p. 380), includes the following statement:

> Dr Albert Ellis' theoretical contributions have had a profound impact on the professional practice of psychology. His theories on the primacy of cognition in psychopathology are at the forefront of practice and research in Clinical Psychology. Dr Ellis' theories have importantly encouraged an active-directive approach to psychological treatment, combined with a deep humanistic respect for the uniqueness of the individual . . . Dr Ellis expanded his clinical work in marital and sex therapy into a comprehensive theory of psychological treatment, Rational-Emotive Therapy. His theories have provided a starting point for many who investigate the nature of human emotional disturbance and its treatment.

By the 1980s, REBT was also having an international impact. Institutes for Rational-Emotive Therapy had been established in Australia, Britain, Canada, Germany, Israel, Italy, Mexico and the Netherlands. Most of these institutes, like the original one founded in New York City, offer training for therapists as well as therapy for clients.

Also in the 1980s, a number of professional books appeared that detailed the application of REBT to a growing number of problem areas and therapeutic modalities. With regard to problem areas, books were published which described REBT's application to alcohol and substance abuse (Ellis, McInerney, DiGiuseppe and Yeager, 1988), anxiety disorders (Warren and Zgourides, 1991) and problems of childhood and adolescence (Ellis and Bernard, 1983; Bernard and Joyce, 1984). With respect to therapeutic modalities, various treatment manuals described means for applying REBT to couples therapy (Ellis, Sichel, Yeager, DiMattia and DiGiuseppe, 1989), family therapy (Huber and Baruth, 1989), and individual counselling (Dryden, 1987a). REBT also found a unique application in Rational Recovery, a self-help group for alcoholics and substance abusers that offers an alternative to the traditional twelve-step programme espoused by Alcoholics Anonymous and Narcotics Anonymous (Ellis and Velten, 1992; Trimpey, 1992).

As always, a good portion of Ellis's professional writings during the 1980s were focused upon explication of the general principles and techniques of REBT. In addition, Ellis presented incisive critiques of a number of widely used therapeutic approaches, and offered his ideas on the resolution of treatment impasses and the maintenance and generalization of therapeutic gains.

With respect to critiques of alternative therapeutic approaches, Ellis (1982, 1983a, 1985a; Ellis and Yeager, 1989) presented his views on techniques and strategies that can tend to be ineffective, inefficient, and iatrogenic for clients (these critiques will be discussed more fully in Chapter 3). Of particular note, he was strongly critical of approaches that encourage individuals to surrender their fates to the hands of some sort of mystical or god-like Higher Power. Such approaches may teach people that they are ultimately powerless to control their own feelings and behaviour, which is a position that runs counter to REBT's advocacy of self-responsibility for emotional problems. Ellis took specific aim at Alcoholics Anonymous as well as transpersonal psychology, and provoked some heated responses from adherents to these approaches.

With regard to the resolution of treatment impasses, Ellis's writings touched upon several important areas. He presented his ideas concerning *discomfort anxiety* (to be discussed in detail in Chapter 2), which he identified as a significant (though not insurmountable) obstacle to change for many clients in therapy (Ellis, 1979b, 1980a, 1987a). He published a series of papers on dealing with resistance in psychotherapy (Ellis, 1983b, c, 1984a, 1985b), which were subsequently consolidated in book form as *Overcoming Resistance* (Ellis, 1985c). He reported research he had conducted which attempted to specifically identify factors contributing to poor outcomes in REBT (Ellis, 1983d) and identified several irrational beliefs that therapists may subscribe to that could compromise treatment effectiveness (Ellis, 1984b). Finally, Ellis (1984c) wrote a pamphlet for clients (which is also instructive for therapists) on 'How to maintain and enhance your rational-emotive therapy gains'. This pamphlet presents backsliding as a common component of the therapeutic change process, and offers clients an arsenal of techniques for dealing with relapses and extending the benefits they have derived from treatment.

Albert Ellis, the Person

Throughout most of his life as a professional psychologist, Albert Ellis has devoted a tremendous amount of energy and time to the development and promulgation of rational emotive behaviour therapy. Despite his advancing age (he turned 80 in 1993), he still maintains an exceptionally busy schedule. By his own report, during his seventy-fifth year, he had over 3000 half-hour and 700 hour-long therapy sessions with clients, delivered sixty talks and workshops for the general public, led five weekly therapy groups and four 9-hour RET intensives, and provided regular supervisory sessions for twelve therapy trainees at the Institute for Rational-Emotive Therapy (Ellis, 1991a). He was the keynote speaker at eight state, national and international psychology conventions, and conducted thirty-five REBT workshops at various locations in the United States. In addition, he published twelve articles and book chapters, as well as three full-length books! His bibliography currently includes a total of approximately fifty-four books, 400 professional articles and 200 audio- and videotapes.

Unquestionably, Ellis is one of the most productive psychologists of this century. In an article entitled 'My philosophy of work and love', he provided the following breakdown of his daily schedule:

8:30 to 9:00 AM: Rise within ten seconds after my alarm rings; wash, dress, eat, and take my daily shot of insulin.[2]

9:00 to 9:30 AM: Confer with our administrator about various business and personnel matters involved with running our two nonprofit institutes.

9:30 AM to 1:00 PM: Conduct individual therapy sessions with clients of the Institute's clinic. Most of my individual sessions during the day run for half an hour, with no breaks in between sessions. But some, especially with couples or families, are hour-long sessions. At 11:30 AM, during one of my sessions, I eat my second meal of the day, a sandwich.

1:00 to 3:00 PM: Supervision at the Institute for Rational-Emotive Therapy's ten or twelve training Fellows, especially in regard to their group therapy participation. Each of these Fellows is in one of my . . . regular therapy groups and assists me in running the group. (Actually, I mainly lead each of the groups for one and a half hours once a week while the training Fellows mainly lead, without me, the second part of the group session, which runs for an additional forty-five minutes.) In the course of this supervision session, I usually eat another sandwich and some fruit, since to balance my daily shot of insulin I consume eight small meals each day. During this supervisory session all kinds of group therapy and other problems are raised and discussed by me and the Fellows. The theory and practice of RET is outlined in regard to the clinical problems that are discussed and attempts are made to refine and develop its main hypotheses.

3:00 to 5:00 PM: Supervision of the individual psychotherapy sessions of three of our training Fellows. They bring to this supervision session tape-recordings of their regular RET interviews with clients for review and discussion. (Sometimes, instead of supervising our training Fellows, I supervise the participants in the Institute's five-day training practica for therapists who come to New York (or to other cities where we give these practica) to work for our Primary Certificate or our Associate Fellowship Certificate in RET.)

5:00 to 5:30 PM: Supper in my apartment on the sixth floor of our building. I usually eat, at this time, one of my two hot meals of the day – sometimes cooked by me and sometimes by the woman I have lived with for almost two decades, Dr Janet L. Wolfe. Oh, yes! – we also talk and share at this time.

5:30 to 6:00 PM: Individual psychotherapy session with one of my regular clinic clients.

6:00 to 7:30 PM: Leading one of my weekly regular therapy groups, with from ten to thirteen group members present and with the assistance of one of our training Fellows.

7:30 to 9:00 PM: Leading another of my regular therapy groups (in the course of which I eat my fifth small meal of the day, usually a cheese sandwich).

9:00 to 11:00 PM: Final half-hour or hour-long individual psychotherapy sessions with some of my regular clinic clients.

11:00 to 11:30 PM: Another hot meal, usually cooked by Janet. Conversation with her about Institute and personal affairs.

11:30 PM to 12:15 AM: Return to my office on the second floor of our building. Finish up Institute business for the day and dictate letters relating to my fairly voluminous world-wide correspondence.

12:15 to 1:00 AM: Return to sixth floor apartment for conversation with Janet, brief physical exercise program, and shower. Usually get to bed by 1:00 AM.

1:00 to 1:15 AM: Final small sandwich before bedtime. Soon sound asleep.

3:30 to 4:10 AM: Spontaneously awake; go to the bathroom; eat my eighth and final sandwich of the day, brush and water-pik my teeth (for the eighth time), and go back to sleep.

8:30 AM: Here I go again for a new day!
(Ellis, 1983e: 48–9)

Ellis acknowledges that ageing has had a slight negative impact on his work habits:

Has older age slowed me down? Yes, a little. I sleep a bit more. I procrastinate slightly on important things while barging ahead with less important ones. I take a few daytime naps on weekends, which I never took in my early life. I spend less time, because of my aching back, sitting up at the typewriter and more time using speedwriting or dictating in my comfortable lounge chair. (Ellis, 1989b: 133)

He has indicated, however, that he has maintained a general routine of beginning work at 9:30 AM and ending at about 11:00 PM for most of his professional life (Yankura and Dryden, 1990).

How has Ellis managed to be so consistently productive across a career spanning approximately fifty years? He provided an answer to this question during a recent interview with the second author of this volume:

> The reason why I've done so much and still, at the age of 75, get so much done is, I would say, largely the result of biology. First, I was born to two highly energetic parents who both lived reasonably long lives and were active until the last days of their lives. So I have a very high energy level, which has made it easier for me to do many more things than others. Second, I have another tendency . . . to get vitally absorbed in what I'm interested in and this, coupled with my high energy, means that it's not hard to do as many things as I do. Other people may neither have a vital absorption in something nor may they have high energy. Third, in many ways I have a very high frustration tolerance. . . . When I write a book, for example, most of it is relatively easy and enjoyable for me to do, but when I come to making up the bibliography, I don't enjoy it as much as it is a pain in the ass to complete. But I just say 'fuck it,' and I sit down and do it. My high frustration tolerance allows me to push through with projects, parts of which I really don't enjoy. (Dryden and Ellis, 1989: 545)

In addition to the traits described above, Ellis (1983e; Dryden and Ellis, 1989; Yankura and Dryden, 1990) has also admitted that he has a tendency to easily become bored when he is not directing his energies toward a challenging, multi-faceted project that involves a long-range goal or purpose. Thus, across most of his adult life, he has minimized the amount of time allotted to common human activities such as socializing, vacationing, engaging in idle chit-chat and availing oneself of entertainments such as plays and movies.

With this tendency to become bored easily, how has Ellis managed to deal with the repetitiveness inherent in practising REBT with a great number of clients? He notes again that he naturally has a rather high tolerance for frustration (and is thus unlikely to internally whine and moan at the prospect of seeing client after client), and states also that he uses his clinical practice as a vehicle for developing the theory and practice of REBT (Ellis, 1972a; Yankura and Dryden, 1990). He has, in fact, published a book chapter describing two separate cases that prompted him to develop his ideas concerning the ideological roots of emotional problems and the importance of attending to clients' discomfort disturbance within therapy (Ellis, 1987b).

Does Ellis ever experience emotional upset? He has indicated that he almost never causes himself to experience anxiety or depression (Weinrach and Ellis, 1980). He admits, however, that he will occasionally make himself angry at other people when, in his view, they act stupidly or unjustly. At such times, he will attempt to constructively deal with his angry feelings by employing the same sorts of rational emotive behavioural techniques that he teaches to his clients. In fact, the reader can find a fairly detailed description of how Ellis dealt with a particular series of emotional upsets he experienced in a book chapter he wrote entitled, 'Psychotherapy without tears' (Ellis, 1972a).

Due to his commitment to his professional work, Ellis has allowed little time for the types of activities that typically contribute to the formation of intimate social relationships. Hence, although he has many acquaintances and amiable working relationships with most of his staff at the Institute, he has few close friendships. Because he is so often task-focused and concerned with utilizing his time as efficiently as feasible, other individuals sometimes regard him as being a cold and brusque person. Windy Dryden, for example, has noted that Ellis can at first seem rather gruff during face-to-face (non-therapy) contacts with colleagues, and that he only gradually appears to warm up to the person with whom he is speaking. Dryden has, however, also noted that Ellis generally comes across as warmer and friendlier in written correspondence. Ellis attributes this to the fact that when he has allotted time in his busy schedule for letter-writing, he tends not to preoccupy himself with other matters (Dryden and Ellis, 1989).

The view that Ellis is a completely cold and brusque person is also belied by the experience of many of the REBT trainees he has supervised over the years. Irwin Altrows, an REBT therapist working in Canada, provided the following illustrative anecdote for a book commemorating Ellis's seventy-fifth birthday entitled, *Will the Real Albert Ellis Please Stand Up?*:

> While working toward the Associate Fellowship Certificate in RET, I was at first hesitant to request supervision from Albert Ellis: What if he were to think I was hopelessly terrible at RET? And if he did think so, would he not say so in a very direct manner, recognizing that people, including aspiring RET practitioners, do not *need* approval?
>   . . . Later, in watching Al supervise others, I started paying attention to his supervisory style, and concluded that he is one of the gentlest supervisors I have seen within or outside of the RET camp. When trainees put themselves down for the quality of their work, he shows them that they are acceptable human beings regardless of their performance. He does not try to demonstrate how clever he can be in spotting errors, but selects one or a few areas where a comment can be helpful and leaves the person with an enhanced sense of efficacy. More than any clinician I have met, he demonstrates the ability to leave unsaid things that are better, at least for the moment, left unsaid. By showing that he can accept us with our imperfections, Albert Ellis inspires us to do the same for ourselves, our trainees, and our clients. (DiMattia and Lega, 1990: 114–15)

In their book, DiMattia and Lega (1990) provide numerous other anecdotes and accolades from Ellis's professional colleagues which attest to his capacity to be humorous, generous and supportive.

Undoubtedly, Ellis's closest and most intimate relationship is with Dr Janet L. Wolfe (an accomplished psychologist and the Executive Director of the Institute for Rational-Emotive Therapy), with whom he has lived since 1965.[3] They initially had what Ellis terms an 'open relationship', which allowed them both to have non-intense involvements with other partners. Over the course of time, however, their relationship evolved into an increasingly monogamous one. Dr Wolfe is certainly a more social being than Ellis, but apparently does not pressure him to share in her social activities. She is also devoted to REBT and the Institute, and has her own professional interests and projects to which she directs a substantial amount of her time. Ellis seems to find the arrangement they share to be ideal, as it allows him to proceed with his work and still reap the benefits of an intimate partnership. In his own words (Dryden and Ellis, 1989: 54), he has stated that 'Janet Wolfe is a beautiful and exceptionally important part of my life, which would be greatly bereft of laughter, warmth, and intimacy without her.'

Ellis has indicated that he and Dr Wolfe mutually chose to have no children. With respect to his own reasons for making this decision, he has offered the following:

> For my part, I would make a lousy father, since I have little interest in taking kids to ball games or picnics and frankly enjoy the various things that I do, especially 'therapizing,' lecturing, giving workshops, and writing, distinctly more than I would enjoy cavorting with children. I would have liked to have had the experience of trying to rear a 'rational' child; but I am skeptical that the child himself or herself would have enjoyed it that much. So my sense of ethics has kept me away from the responsibility of being a full-time father. I nurture, in my own way, my many clients; and that makes up for my lack of being a conventional family man. (Ellis, 1991a: 21)

Albert Ellis, in addition to being an outstanding psychotherapist and theoretician, is also in many ways a most unusual human being. Far more than the vast majority of people, he has derived his life's satisfaction from an intense devotion to a single (but multi-faceted) large-scale project: the growth of rational emotive behaviour therapy. He has probably helped thousands of suffering individuals through his self-help materials, lectures, and therapy sessions; and he has had a profound impact on the fields of psychotherapy and counselling. He almost single-handedly brought REBT to the forefront of contemporary approaches to therapy, and played a major role in bringing about the cognitive-behavioural revolution within mental health practice. He stands as an inspiring model of frustration tolerance, goal-directedness and rational thinking.

Notes

1 Ellis has also received many other professional and academic awards, including membership in the National Academies of Practice and the major Professional Development Award of the American Counseling Association. He holds the Humanist of the Year Award of the American Humanist Association and the Distinguished Alumni Awards at the City College of New York and Teachers College, Columbia University.
2 Ellis has diabetes. Because of this, he has kept to a strict regimen with respect to his diet and insulin injections.
3 Ellis's relationship with Dr Wolfe has been the most enduring one of his life. He has, however, been married twice in the past. He was briefly married to Karyl Corper in 1939, but they had their marriage annulled. He married Rhoda Winter, a dancer, in 1956, and had a mutually satisfying relationship with her for two and a half years. They became incompatible and got divorced after she became less involved with her dancing and wanted to spend much more time with Ellis and their friends.

2

Major Contributions to Theory

Largely on the basis of my clinical experimentation, I forged ahead in the early 1950s to discover the gross ineffectuality of psychoanalysis and to develop more rational and distinctly more efficient techniques with my clients. And as I did so, I began to develop RET theory.

(Ellis, 1977b: 4)

Overview

At the outset, it is worthwhile to recognize that Albert Ellis's original formulation of the theory of rational emotive behaviour therapy grew out of several important influences: his readings of both ancient and contemporary philosophers; his exposure to the work of other psychotherapists and personality theorists; and his own life experiences. REBT thus represents a synthesis of a number of disparate ideas and concepts. Perhaps more so than many other theoreticians, Ellis has been quite specific in identifying or describing these influences.

With respect to philosophical influences, Ellis's formulation of REBT drew from the work of both ancient and contemporary philosophers. In the former category, Ellis has acknowledged the writings of ancient Greek and Roman Stoic philosophers, particularly those of Epictetus and Marcus Aurelius. In fact, Epictetus's famous dictum – 'People are disturbed not by things, but by the view which they take of them' – is frequently quoted within the REBT literature since it encapsulates one of the basic tenets of this approach to therapy. With respect to more modern philosophical influences, Ellis has cited the work of individuals such as Kant, Popper and Russell. Ellis has also indicated that he was influenced by the work of certain existential philosophers (for example, Martin Heidegger and Paul Tillich) and general semanticists (for example, Alfred Korzybski). Hence, REBT can be contrasted with other schools of therapy insofar as it has a very strong and explicit philosophical foundation.

Ellis has also acknowledged that his ideas were influenced by the work of a number of contemporary psychotherapists. Alfred Adler's (1927) Individual Psychology, for instance, stressed the importance of focusing upon the philosophies, values and personal goals of individuals. Karen Horney (1950) coined the term 'tyranny of the shoulds', which refers to neurotic demands that people may self-defeatingly impose on themselves. In addition, Ellis's nascent formulation of REBT was influenced by the ideas and experiments of some of the early behaviourists (Watson and Rayner, 1920; Jones, 1924), which involved *in vivo* exposure to feared stimuli as a means for overcoming phobias.

Ellis's experience in overcoming his shyness earlier in life also played a hand in determining his eventual formulation of rational emotive behaviour therapy. As described in the preceding chapter, he found that philosophically based interventions, combined with active exposure to feared situations, ultimately proved most beneficial in terms of helping him to conquer his fear of rejection. Also, Ellis's experience as a practising psychoanalyst, and his subsequent experimentation with alternative therapeutic approaches, heavily impacted upon the form that his theory of psychotherapy would take.

While the theory underpinning rational emotive behaviour therapy is certainly multi-faceted, its essence can be quickly grasped by reducing it to several fundamental hypotheses which can be abstracted from Ellis's writings. These hypotheses are as follows (Ellis, 1976a, 1977b, 1979c, 1984d; Ellis and Dryden, 1990):

1 Human beings have a biologically based tendency to create and subscribe to deeply held beliefs about themselves, other people and the world around them.
2 These beliefs can importantly influence emotions and behaviours (and also other types of cognitions and cognitive processes).
3 Certain types of beliefs will contribute to self-enhancing, goal-promoting emotions and behaviours; other sorts of beliefs will contribute to self-defeating emotions and behaviours.
4 It is possible to identify and modify the sorts of beliefs that contribute to self-defeating emotions and behaviours.
5 Modification of these beliefs can help an individual to be less vulnerable to emotional disturbances and dysfunctional behaviour.
6 Since these beliefs are often deeply rooted within an individual's personality, modification of them can involve a significant amount of ongoing and consistent effort.

The sections that follow will present essential details on these hypotheses, such that the reader will be provided with a fuller understanding of rational-emotive theory. In particular, the material in this chapter will: (a) distinguish between the types of beliefs that contribute to either psychological disturbance or health, (b) present Ellis's views on the nature of psychological disturbance, (c) describe Ellis's model for conceptualizing episodes of emotional disturbances, (d) present criteria for psychological health and (e) describe Ellis's perspective on the process of therapeutic change.

Psychological Disturbance and Health: The Role of Beliefs

Ellis, from the outset, recognized that human beings seem to have an innate tendency or drive to try and make sense of the world in which they exist. In this sense he agrees with George Kelly's (1955) view of human beings as 'scientists'. We are constantly advancing hypotheses about ourselves, other people and our environment, in an attempt to increase our understanding of the world and thus live as happily and comfortably as possible. In Ellis's terms, these hypotheses are referred to as 'beliefs'. Collectively, our beliefs can be viewed as constituting a 'philosophy of life'.

Scientists recognize that the hypotheses that make up their scientific theories need to be tested in order to determine if they have any validity. Unfortunately, human beings frequently neglect to test the beliefs that comprise their personal philosophies of life. As a result, they may continue to utilize a particular belief as a guiding principle even when it leads them into all sorts of emotional and behavioural difficulties.

Ellis and other REBT therapists teach clients to recognize that they may be holding certain dysfunctional beliefs, and show them how to challenge, discard and replace these beliefs such that they become less vulnerable to significant emotional upsets and self-defeating behaviour.

Rational versus Irrational Beliefs

Ellis (1962, 1973a, 1979c; Ellis and Harper, 1975) distinguishes between two basic types of beliefs in his discussions of psychological disturbance and health. *Rational* (or functional) beliefs are viewed as contributing to the individual's welfare, satisfaction and happiness, while *irrational* (or dysfunctional) beliefs are seen as contributing to significant episodes of emotional disturbance and dysfunctional behaviour. According to Ellis, it is possible to contrast rational and irrational beliefs on a number of different dimensions.

Demandingness. Irrational beliefs embody absolutistic, rigid demands, and can be verbally expressed in the form of 'shoulds', 'musts', 'have to's' and 'ought to's'. Rational beliefs, on the other hand, merely reflect an individual's preferences, wants, desires and wishes. The statement, 'I *must* have the love and approval of my significant others' could be considered an irrational belief (when it is understood that the 'must' connotes an absolutistic demand about a particular life condition), while the phrase, 'I *want* the love and approval of my significant others, but I don't *need* this' would usually be regarded as a rational belief.

Verifiability. Irrational beliefs are almost always empirically inconsistent with reality. Thus, they can often be refuted by making reference to the way things generally appear to be in the real world. The 'must' described in the preceding paragraph on 'demandingness' would be considered inconsistent with reality, as evidence could be cited to demonstrate that it is not an utter necessity for adult human beings to be loved by those they consider significant – they can survive, and still be happy, even without such love. Rational beliefs generally tend to be more in consonance with reality.

Logical Consistency. Rational beliefs are usually logically consistent, as in the following example: 'It is good to be successful at one's job; therefore, I *want* to be successful at *my* job.' Most people would probably agree that the second part of this sentence follows logically from the first part. Contrast this sentence, however, with another sentence: 'It is good to be successful at one's job; therefore, I absolutely *must* be successful at mine.' This is an illogical *non sequitur*, as that which is desirable doesn't absolutely *have to* be.

Emotional and Behavioural Consequences. According to Ellis, irrational beliefs will make individuals more vulnerable to unwanted emotional and behavioural effects, or consequences. Thus, individuals who believe, 'I *must* become a talented musician in order to consider myself a worthwhile person', may very well engage in negative self-evaluation and experience depression (an undesirable emotional consequence) if their goal is not realized. Their depression could conceivably contribute to extreme social withdrawal (an undesirable behavioural consequence). Rational beliefs are less likely to lead individuals into such problematic feeling states as depression, anxiety, guilt, shame and anger.

In some of his earlier presentations of rational emotive behaviour therapy, Ellis (1962; Ellis and Harper, 1975) provided a list of the major irrational beliefs to which human beings may subscribe. This list, which he based upon his clinical experience with therapy clients, included the following items.

Irrational Idea no. 1: One *must* have love and approval from all of the people one finds significant.

Irrational Idea no. 2: One *must* prove thoroughly competent and achieving; or, at the very least, one *must* have talent or competence in some important area.

Irrational Idea no. 3: When other people act obnoxiously and unfairly, one should blame and damn them, and view them as bad, wicked or rotten individuals.

Irrational Idea no. 4: One *must* view things as awful, terrible, horrible, and catastrophic when one is seriously frustrated, treated unfairly or rejected.

Irrational Idea no. 5: Emotional misery comes from external pressures and one has little ability to control or change one's feelings.

Irrational Idea no. 6: If something seems dangerous or fearsome, one *must* be preoccupied with it and make oneself anxious about it.

Irrational Idea no. 7: It is easier to avoid than to face life's difficulties and responsibilities, rather than undertaking more rewarding forms of self-discipline.

Irrational Idea no. 8: The past remains all-important; the fact that something once strongly influenced one's life means that it *has to* keep determining one's feelings and behaviours in the present day.

Irrational Idea no. 9: People and things *should* turn out better than they do; it *must* be viewed as awful and horrible if one does not find good solutions to life's problems.

Irrational Idea no. 10: One can achieve maximum happiness through inertia and inaction or by passively and uncommittedly 'enjoying oneself'.

In more recent discussions of irrational beliefs, rather than presenting a list of such beliefs, Ellis (Ellis and Bernard, 1985; Ellis and Dryden, 1987) has emphasized that they can be applied to self, other people or conditions as they exist in the world. This

alternative way of conceptualizing irrational beliefs allows counsellors and therapists greater fluidity with respect to identifying the
main shoulds, musts and oughts to which their clients subscribe.

In addition to affecting a person's emotional and behavioural
consequences, irrational beliefs may also influence other cognitive
processes and cognitions. Ellis (1984d) has noted that when
individuals adhere to absolute shoulds and musts, they will often
tend to lead themselves to a number of irrational conclusions which
are viewed as derivatives of their original irrational beliefs. He has
termed these derivatives 'awfulizing', 'I-can't-stand-it-itis' and
'damnation'. 'Awfulizing' refers to evaluating conditions as being
more than 100 per cent bad when they are not as they 'must' be. 'I-
can't-stand-it-itis' involves rating conditions as absolutely intoler-
able (and as totally eclipsing any possibility of happiness or
satisfaction) if an event that 'must' not occur actually does occur or
threatens to occur. 'Damnation' refers to negative person-rating.
When we fail to achieve or attain that which we believe we 'must'
have, we will tend to globally condemn or damn ourselves. When
other people fail to provide us with what we believe we 'must' have
from them (for example, love, support, respect) we will likely
condemn or damn *them* in a global sense. As with musts and
shoulds, Ellis holds that these irrational derivatives will lead
individuals to experience significant upsets and engage in dysfunctional behaviours.

A number of cognitive-behavioural theorists (notably Beck, 1976;
Beck, Rush, Shaw and Emery, 1979; Beck and Emery, 1985) have
emphasized the role played by negatively distorted inferences in the
genesis of emotional disturbance. The term 'inferences' is here used
to refer mainly to the interpretations, causal attributions and
predictions that people apply to their perceptions of their life
conditions, their own behaviour and the behaviour of others (see
Dryden and Yankura, 1993). While rational-emotive theory
acknowledges that negatively distorted inferences can be *involved*
in episodes of emotional disturbance, it does not assign them
primacy with respect to causation. Ellis notes that inferences are
generally non-evaluative in nature, and stresses that cognitions of
an *evaluative* nature (that is, irrational beliefs and their associated
derivatives) are usually at the root of most self-defeating emotions
and behaviours. Importantly, Ellis has suggested that distorted
inferences actually stem from irrational beliefs. In his own words,
he has stated that 'For the most part . . . you tend, as a human, to
make antiempirical overgeneralizations because you have a hidden
*must*urbatory agenda in your thinking' (Ellis, 1977b: 9). Thus, an
individual who subscribes to the irrational belief, 'I *must* have the

love and approval of my friends', may be more likely to infer total dislike and disapproval from significant others when they even slightly deviate from accepting, caring behaviours. A number of experiments completed by Dryden and associates (Dryden, Ferguson and Clark, 1989; Dryden, Ferguson and Hylton, 1989; Dryden, Ferguson and McTeague, 1989) provide some empirical support for Ellis's contention that negatively distorted inferences tend to follow from irrational beliefs.

Ellis's Views on the Nature of Human Psychological Disturbance

As the foregoing section indicates, Ellis accords irrational beliefs a place of central importance with respect to the origins of psychological disturbance. In his writings, he has made a number of additional points concerning this issue. In particular, he has posited that (a) humans have a biologically based tendency to engage in irrational thinking (Ellis, 1976a); (b) a distinction can be made between the types of emotions stemming from irrational beliefs vs. rational beliefs (Ellis and Dryden, 1987); and (c) it is possible to identify two fundamental types of psychological disturbance: ego disturbance and discomfort disturbance (Ellis, 1979b, 1980a). The sections that follow will elaborate on each of these points.

The Biological Basis of Human Irrationality

Most major theories of psychotherapy (for example, psychoanalysis and social learning theory) maintain that environmental conditions and learning experiences are the major determinants of psychological disturbance. While Ellis acknowledges that factors external to the individual most probably play a part in contributing to either psychological disturbance or health, he strongly believes that human beings have a biologically based tendency to construct (and adhere to) irrational beliefs that can lead them to self-defeating emotional and behavioural consequences (Ellis, 1976a). This emphasis upon a biological basis for irrational thinking and psychological disturbance was quite unique when Ellis first presented it in the 1950s, especially considering that psychoanalysis (with its focus upon upbringing and childhood experiences) was the prevalent form of therapy at that time. Even in the present day, most 'competing' psychotherapy theorists tend to focus more on social conditioning factors.

What does Ellis mean by the phrase 'biological basis' with reference to irrational thinking? He has explained it as follows:

By *biological basis* I mean that a characteristic or trait has distinctly innate (as well as distinctly acquired) origins – it partly arises from the organism's natural, easy predisposition to behave in certain stipulated ways. I do not mean that this characteristic or trait has a purely instinctive basis, that it cannot undergo major change, nor that the organism would perish, or at least live in abject misery, without it. I simply mean that, because of its genetic and/or congenital nature, an individual easily develops this trait and has a difficult time modifying or eliminating it. (Ellis, 1977b: 14–15)

Ellis's position on the biological basis of human irrational thinking is based upon his observations of clients within therapy, as well as his knowledge of the broader social contexts within which humans exist. He offers the following observations as support for his views in this regard (Ellis, 1976a):

1 Virtually all human beings, including very bright and capable people, manifest evidence of adhering to particular irrationalities. Ellis (1977b: 15) has written, 'do you know anyone who has remained perfectly free of all neurotic symptoms, never subscribed to religious dogmas, and never surrendered to any foolish health habits? I practically defy you to come up with a single case!'

2 Just about all of the disturbance-creating irrational beliefs found in our society can be found, in one form or another, in probably all of the social and cultural groups that have ever been studied. Ellis (1977b: 15) notes that 'Although rules, laws, mores, and standards vary widely from group to group, gullibility, absolutism, dogmas, religiosity, and demandingness *about* these standards remain surprisingly similar.'

3 Many of the irrational beliefs to which people subscribe go counter to the *sensible* teachings of parents, teachers and other influences.

4 Even when bright and competent individuals give up one set of irrational beliefs, they can fairly often tend to adopt a new set of irrationalities. Thus, as Ellis (1977b: 17) has observed, 'Devout religionists often turn into devout atheists ... Individuals who procrastinate mightily may later emerge as compulsive workers ... Extremism tends to remain as a natural human trait that takes one foolish form or another.'

5 Even individuals who *usually* tend to think rationally will sometimes revert to irrational beliefs (and their behavioural concomitants) at certain times. Ellis (1977b: 17) notes that 'unusual environmental conditions often bring out silly behavior by normally sane individuals. But these individuals obviously react to these conditions because they have some

basic disposition to go out of their heads under unusual kinds of stress – and that disposition probably has innate elements.'

6 Human beings who are highly opposed to particular irrationalities can often fall prey to these very same irrationalities. 'Agnostics give in to devout, absolutistic thoughts and feelings. Highly religious individuals act quite immorally. Psychologists who believe that guilt or self-downing has no legitimacy make themselves guilty and self-downing' (Ellis, 1977b: 17).

7 Insight into one's own irrational thinking may have no effect or only a partial effect in helping one to surrender that type of thinking. Ellis (1977b: 18) has written that 'This largely arises from the human tendency to have two contradictory beliefs at the same time – an "intellectual" one which you lightly and occasionally hold and an "emotional" one which you vigorously and consistently hold and which you therefore usually tend to act upon. This tendency to have simultaneous contradictory beliefs again seems part of the human condition.'

8 People often will revert back to irrational patterns of thinking, even after they have worked quite hard (in psychotherapy, for example) to overcome them.

9 Human beings often appear to learn self-defeating behaviours more readily than self-enhancing behaviours. 'Thus, they very easily overeat but have great trouble sticking to a sensible diet. They can learn, usually from their foolish peers, to smoke cigarettes; but if other peers or elders try to teach them to give up smoking or to act more self-disciplinedly in other ways, they resist this teaching to a fare-thee-well!' (Ellis, 1977b: 19–20).

10 Individuals can tend to construct irrational beliefs that are based on their own very strong feelings about something. These beliefs do not appear to be learned from any particular source or authority. Thus, a person may believe that she'll love a particular partner 'forever' at the early stages of a relationship, simply because she has such strong love feelings for that partner in the present time. She subscribes to this belief despite her knowledge that infatuation is almost always a transient stage within a relationship.

11 Many forms of irrational thinking appear to represent gross overgeneralizations. 'Thus, you easily start with a sensible observation, "I failed at that test," and then you overgeneralize to "I will always fail; I have no ability to succeed at it"' (Ellis, 1977b: 19). Such overgeneralizations seem to be a frequent, naturally occurring aspect of humans' cognitive functioning.

As noted in Chapter 1, a theory of psychotherapy which holds that the main determinant of psychological disturbance has biologically based roots carries important implications for the actual practice of therapy. Ellis (1979d, 1985c) has noted, for instance, that it is advisable for therapists to dispute their clients' irrational beliefs in a vigorous and persistent manner. The issue of applying force and energy in the service of bringing about beneficial cognitive modifications will receive further treatment in Chapter 3.

Two Categories of Emotional Consequences
As noted earlier, irrational and rational beliefs will lead individuals to experience different sorts of emotional consequences. Irrational beliefs will generally contribute to episodes of *unhealthy negative emotions*, while rational beliefs will usually result in *healthy negative emotions*.[1] Ellis uses the terms 'unhealthy' and 'healthy' to describe these two categories of emotional consequences because the feeling states stemming from rational beliefs can be considered a *healthy* (that is, reasonable, potentially self-helping) response to undesirable conditions and outcomes, while the feeling states that tend to follow from irrational beliefs represent an *unhealthy* (that is, extreme, potentially self-defeating) response to undesirable conditions and outcomes. Unhealthy negative emotions include states such as anger, anxiety, depression, guilt and shame. These can be contrasted with the healthy negative emotions of annoyance, concern, sadness, remorse and regret (see Dryden and Yankura, 1993, for a detailed discussion of the cognitive and behavioural concomitants of these differing emotional states).

To clarify the posited relationship between type of belief and the type of emotional consequence an individual experiences, an example will be provided. Consider the hypothetical case of Elizabeth, a young woman who is married to Arthur. Both of these individuals are employed outside of the home during the day; however, because Arthur's job allows him to arrive home one and a half hours before Elizabeth, he has the responsibility of preparing the evening meal. Unfortunately, he is sometimes lax in meeting this responsibility and frequently doesn't start cooking until shortly before Elizabeth is due in. Hence, dinner is often 'late'.

Elizabeth can mainly subscribe to either a rational belief or an irrational belief about Arthur's 'procrastination with the pots'. If she mainly subscribes to the rational belief, 'I strongly *wish* that Arthur would have dinner ready on time, but he doesn't *have to* do so – it's only inconvenient and hardly the end of the world if dinner is late', she would tend to feel merely disappointed and annoyed the next time her spouse runs behind schedule in getting dinner on the table. Her disappointment and annoyance would be considered healthy negative emotions since, although they are negative in tone, they represent a reasonable reaction to unwanted circumstances and are unlikely to lead to self-defeating behaviours. In fact, Elizabeth's feelings of disappointment and annoyance could actually contribute to self-helping behaviours, insofar as they may motivate her to assertively (not aggressively) request that Arthur attempt to mend his ways.

If, however, Elizabeth escalates her rational preference to the level of an absolutistic demand (that is, an irrational belief), she will, according to Ellis and REBT theory, be much more likely to experience an unhealthy negative emotion. Thus, if she subscribes to the belief, 'Arthur absolutely *must* have dinner ready on time tonight; if he doesn't, he's a totally inconsiderate loser', she may very well respond to Arthur's next failure with a feeling of raging anger. This feeling, in turn, could contribute to verbally aggressive behaviour (that is, sharp criticisms and accusations) which may only make a bad situation worse.

To summarize, when conditions are not (or potentially may not be) as an individual would *like* them to be (in accordance with his or her rational belief), that individual will most likely experience a healthy negative emotion (for example, disappointment or annoyance) which may motivate him or her to engage in self-helping behaviour. If, on the other hand, an individual brings an irrational belief (that is, an absolutistic should or must with its associated derivatives) to bear upon unwanted conditions, that individual will probably experience an unhealthy negative emotion (for example, depression or raging anger). Compared to its healthy counterpart, this emotion will 'feel' worse in a subjective sense and may lead the individual to engage in self-defeating behaviour.

Based on the foregoing description, the reader will note that there can be a relationship between the type of emotion a person experiences (healthy or unhealthy) and the type of behaviour they may then be likely to engage in (self-helping versus self-defeating). Dryden and Yankura (1993) describe a model wherein particular feeling states prime an individual to have certain 'action tendencies'. These action tendencies may or may not lead the individual to engage in particular categories of behaviour (for example, avoidance; withdrawal), depending upon conditions present in the environment and other relevant aspects of the individual's belief system.

It is also important to note that Ellis posits some specific relationships between the nature of a person's irrational beliefs and the type of unhealthy negative emotion they may be likely to experience (Ellis and Dryden, 1987). Thus, irrational beliefs applied to oneself (for example, 'I *shouldn't* have been so inconsiderate to Mary') can make one vulnerable to feelings such as guilt and shame. When such beliefs are applied to the behaviour of other people (for example, 'He *shouldn't* have criticized me so harshly!'), they can lead to angry, raging feelings. Irrational beliefs applied to unwanted future conditions (for example, 'I *must* not be fired from my job!') can result in feelings of anxiety.

Two Major Categories of Psychological Disturbance
As noted earlier, irrational beliefs can be directed at oneself, other people or conditions as they exist (or *may* exist) in the world. Through his long experience as a practising psychotherapist, Ellis (1979b, 1980a; Dryden and Ellis, 1987) has noted that such beliefs result in two main forms of psychological disturbance: *ego disturbance* and *discomfort disturbance*. These two categories can be viewed as subsuming almost all of the emotional/behavioural problems that clients may present in therapy.

Ego disturbance can result when individuals place absolutistic demands upon themselves (for example, 'I *must* perform well during my orals defence!') and then consequently engage in negative self-rating when they fail in some sense to live up to their rigid, self-imposed demands (for example, 'I didn't answer all of the examiner's questions perfectly as I *should* have; that makes me an incompetent, worthless person!'). *Ego anxiety* can result when people perceive that they may not be able to meet their self-imposed demands in the future. *Ego depression* may be the outcome after the fact, when people perceive that they have indeed failed to live up to the standard they demand of themselves.

Discomfort disturbance may be experienced when individuals apply absolutistic demands to conditions that relate to personal comfort and safety. Thus, a person who believes that he absolutely *should* be able to lose unwanted weight with a minimum of discomfort and effort will be likely to make himself disturbed about the frustrations inherent in dieting. Ellis (1979b, 1980a) originally referred only to discomfort *anxiety* (that is, anxiety stemming from the anticipation of discomfort that one believes *must* not occur) in his writings on this topic; he subsequently broadened the term to 'discomfort disturbance' when he saw that other types of emotional problems (for example, discomfort depression) can also result from applying irrational beliefs to the phenomenon of personal discomfort (Dryden and Ellis, 1987).

As will be seen later in this chapter, the psychologically healthy alternative to ego disturbance is founded upon a philosophy of unconditional self-acceptance (USA). Persons who subscribe to such a philosophy refuse to apply global ratings to themselves, instead preferring to accept themselves as fallible human beings with both positive *and* negative qualities. The psychologically healthy alternative to discomfort disturbance is based upon a philosophy of high frustration (or discomfort) tolerance, wherein one recognizes that uncomfortable conditions are not absolutely awful and can be tolerated in the service of attaining valued goals.

Having presented Ellis's views on major aspects of human psychological disturbance, we next present his framework for understanding and analysing episodes of emotional disturbance. Termed the 'ABC model', it is a cornerstone of the theory and practice of REBT.

Conceptualizing Episodes of Emotional Disturbance: The ABC Model

REBT is famous for Ellis's (1977b; Ellis and Harper, 1975) ABC model, which is a device used for conceptualizing episodes of emotional disturbance and dysfunctional behaviour. In the most simplified form of this model, A stands for 'activating event', and refers to an individual's perceptions and inferences concerning the events and conditions that impact upon him or her. B connotes 'beliefs', and includes both the rational and irrational beliefs that the individual brings to bear upon specific activating events. C stands for 'emotional consequences' (and can also include behavioural consequences), and refers to the emotional (and behavioural) outcomes that the individual experiences as a result of holding particular beliefs at B.

To illustrate the basic relationships between the components of the ABC model, consider the following hypothetical example: Jane has applied for a teaching job at the local university, and has to give a lecture in front of the staff as part of the process of being reviewed as a candidate for the position. She strongly *desires* to do well at this task, as she very much wants to be hired. Thus, she holds the following *rational belief*: 'I strongly *want* to deliver an excellent lecture, as this will carry me a step further on my quest for an academic position.' Unfortunately, she changes her rational desire to the level of an absolute demand, and thus constructs an irrational belief: 'It will benefit me if I do well; therefore, I *must* deliver a first-class lecture!' Now, when she considers the possibility that she might do a less than exemplary job (and perhaps as a result receive poor reviews by the faculty), she feels anxious.

In this example, Jane's thoughts about the possibility that she may do poorly at her upcoming 'audition' constitute her activating event. Note that in this case the activating event is not something that has actually already occurred, it is an anticipated possible future event. This activating event serves to trigger her beliefs at B, namely, (a) 'I *want* to do well' and (b) 'Therefore, I *must* do well.' She then experiences the emotional consequences of anxiety, which could conceivably lead to the behavioural consequences of compulsive over-preparation for the lecture (that is, 'warding off' behaviour). Figure 2.1 provides a graphic illustration of Jane's emotional episode.

Ellis's ABC model has considerable value for both clinicians and clients alike (Yankura and Dryden, 1990). For clinicians, it provides an efficient means for conceptualizing clients' emotional problems, so that effective intervention can begin more quickly than in many other forms of therapy. When therapists and counsellors teach the model to their clients, these individuals can then use it on an independent basis to gain a helpful understanding of the origins of their upsets. This understanding can lead them to view their emotional and behavioural problems as more manageable, and can pave the way for constructive efforts at self-help.

The illustration of the ABC model presented above was quite simplified and unidirectional (that is, activating event —→ beliefs —→ emotional consequences), and does not provide a sense of some of the more complex inter-relationships that can exist between activating events, cognitions and emotions. The two sections that follow will provide details on certain of these inter-relationships.

Secondary Problems: A Special Case of ABC Inter-relationships

Ellis (1984d; Ellis and Bernard, 1985) emphasizes that individuals can create secondary emotional problems about their initial (or primary) emotional problems. According to the ABC model, this occurs when a person's primary emotional consequence becomes an activating event that triggers an additional ABC sequence. Secondary problems can be viewed as 'problems about problems'. Thus, to cite a few of the possibilities, individuals can make themselves depressed about their anxiety, guilty about their anger or ashamed about their depression.

Again, we will offer an example to illustrate the origin of secondary problems. In the case described earlier, Jane made herself anxious with regard to her upcoming presentation by subscribing to the irrational belief, 'I *must* deliver a first-class lecture!' She conceivably could create a secondary emotional problem by taking note of the fact that she is anxious (her initial emotional problem); making this into a new activating event ('Oh, I see that I'm anxious

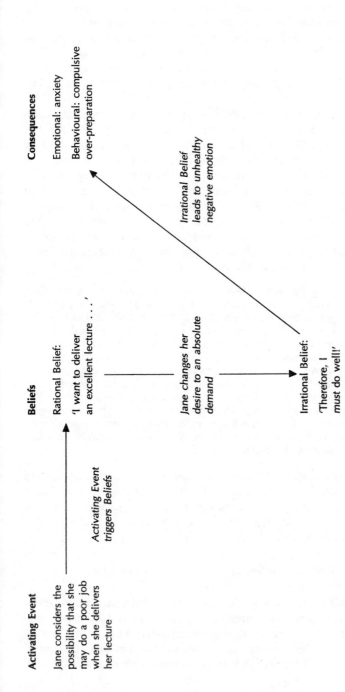

Figure 2.1 Jane's emotional episode as conceptualized with the ABC model

about giving my lecture!'); applying a second irrational belief to this new A ('I *must* not feel so anxious, since my anxiety will prove that I am no good!'); and experiencing a new C of additional anxiety (or 'anxiety about anxiety'). This additional anxiety, of course, will most likely make it ever more difficult for her to focus her efforts on the task in hand. Figure 2.2 outlines Jane's secondary emotional problem.

Unlike many other theorists, Ellis places a unique emphasis upon identifying and remediating clients' secondary problems (Ellis and Bernard, 1985; Dryden and Ellis, 1987). Ellis, in fact, advocates a policy of attempting (whenever feasible) to *first* help clients to overcome their secondary problem, in order that they might then be better able to constructively focus their efforts on dealing with their primary problems (see Dryden, 1990a, for a discussion on how to assess and when to treat clients' secondary problems). The following brief excerpt, drawn from one of Ellis's sessions with a highly anxious woman, illustrates how he will sometimes address secondary problems with clients:

> *Ellis*: Let's go through the ABC's of your problems very clearly. First, you have your original issue: 'If I screw up at work, I'm a shit.' 'A' is the activating event of having to complete some task at work. 'B' is, 'I *must* not screw up; I *must* do a great job and make a good impression on the boss.' Then 'C' is anxiety. Right?
>
> *Client*: That sounds right.
>
> *Ellis*: Now you take 'C' – your anxiety – and you make it into a new 'A'! At 'B', you say to yourself, 'I *must* not be anxious – that would be awful!' Then 'C' becomes anxiety about anxiety! You see, you produce a secondary symptom by doing the same thing on two levels. Now, we want to undo those two symptoms, so we'll start with the secondary anxiety. Why *must* you not be anxious? (Yankura and Dryden, 1990: 45)

Ellis's question at the end of this excerpt is meant to prompt the client to challenge the irrational belief behind her secondary anxiety. Procedures for challenging and replacing irrational beliefs will be described in detail in the section of this chapter on the process of therapeutic change.

Additional ABC Inter-relationships: Advanced Variations on a Theme

From REBT's inception in the mid-1950s, Ellis has acknowledged that activating events, cognitions and emotions can influence each other and often overlap in significant ways. In a recent article published in the *Journal of Rational-Emotive and Cognitive-Behavior Therapy*, Ellis (1991b) presented a revised and expanded

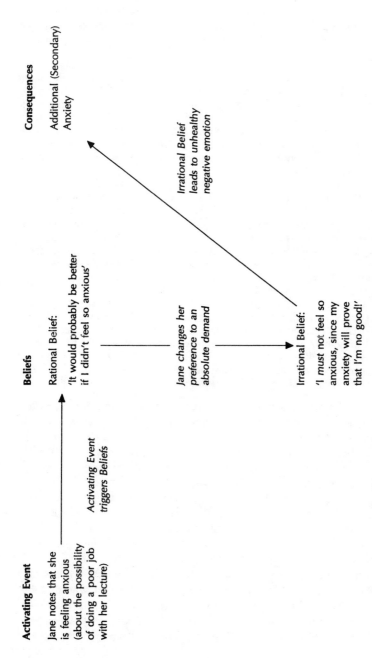

Activating Event

Jane notes that she is feeling anxious (about the possibility of doing a poor job with her lecture)

Activating Event triggers Beliefs

Beliefs

Rational Belief:

'It would probably be better if I didn't feel so anxious'

Jane changes her preference to an absolute demand

Irrational Belief:

'I *must* not feel so anxious, since my anxiety will prove that I'm no good!'

Irrational Belief leads to unhealthy negative emotion

Consequences

Additional (Secondary) Anxiety

Figure 2.2 *Jane's secondary emotional problem*

version of his ABC framework that detailed some of the more complex inter-relationships of A's, B's and C's. While it is beyond the scope of this chapter to provide a complete review of the many ways in which the components of the ABC model can interact, some excerpts from Ellis's article will serve to provide a sense of this:

> The relationships between Activating Events (A's) and Beliefs (B's) about these A's are interactional and reciprocal. A's often significantly influence B's, and B's also often significantly influence A's. Thus, if A is perceived as loss of approval, the Belief, 'I prefer to be approved but I don't have to be,' can influence a person to perceive A as a slight affront, while the Belief 'I must be approved and I'm worthless if I am not!' can influence a person to perceive A as a cruelly intended, persistent, enormous assault.
>
> Similarly, the frequency, kind and degree of the Activating Events (A's) one experiences may easily influence or contribute to one's Beliefs. Thus, if one's behavior is occasionally lightly criticized by another person, one may Believe, 'I'd like this other to approve of me, but if he doesn't it's slightly bad and I can easily stand it.' If, however, one's same behavior is continually heavily excoriated and one is strongly attacked (A) for it, one may construct the Belief, 'This criticism (A) is unfair and must not exist! I can't stand it! My attacker is a rotten person for treating me this way! . . .'
>
> Consequences (C's) also significantly influence or even create A's. Thus, if a woman feels horrified and self-hating about her lover's 'rejecting' her, she may fairly easily see (interpret) him as 'rejecting' (A) when he may actually only be focused on something else. She can even feel so horrified (C) about his rejection (A) that she falsely and defensively sees (interprets) him, at point A, rejecting her when he is really acting indifferently or acceptingly. (Ellis, 1991b: 146–7)

The overlapping, interactional nature of activating events, beliefs and emotional consequences carries important implications for the practice of counselling and psychotherapy. Within REBT, it leads to a multi-modal emphasis with respect to the techniques employed in the service of therapeutic change. REBT's multi-modal emphasis will receive further treatment below.

Having reviewed Ellis's ABC model and his fundamental views on the nature of psychological disturbance, we turn now to consideration of his views on the nature of psychological health.

Criteria for Psychological Health

Ellis hypothesizes that absolutistic shoulds and musts are strongly implicated in psychological disturbance. He holds that when human beings give up their absolutistic philosophies and adhere instead to a probabilistic, preferential philosophy of living, they will make themselves much less vulnerable to dysfunctional emotions and behaviours. They will, however, still experience healthy negative emotions (for example, sadness, disappointment, annoyance) when for some reason they are blocked from having their desires and preferences fulfilled. Healthy negative emotions are viewed as often contributing to constructive psychological functioning, as they can have beneficial motivational properties. They can, for instance, help people to work effectively at removing obstacles to goal attainment. When removal of such obstacles is not possible, these healthy negative emotions can assist individuals in making constructive adjustments to less than optimal circumstances.

In addition to advocating a probabilistic, preferential philosophy of living, Ellis has advanced thirteen tenets which he regards as criteria for psychological health (Ellis, 1967, 1987c; Ellis and Bernard, 1985). Individuals who mainly tend to think probabilistically and who refrain from escalating their desires and preferences to the level of absolutistic demands are probably better able to approach these criteria.

Self-interest. Emotionally healthier people practice what Ellis refers to as enlightened self-interest. This means that they tend to put their own interests and goals first most of the time, while putting those of others, particularly significant others, a close second. Individuals who practise enlightened self-interest may also sometimes choose to put others' desires before their own, especially when the welfare and happiness of others is of great importance to them. Ellis cautions against slavish self-sacrifice; self-sacrifice can, however, be regarded as healthy when a person *wants* to sacrifice his or her own interests and derives personal meaning and happiness from doing so.

Social Interest. Recognizing that human beings are social animals who are generally predisposed to live in groups and seek the company of others, Ellis maintains that psychologically healthier individuals hold to a philosophy of social interest. This means that they choose to usually act morally, protect the rights of others and abet the survival of the community, as doing so will help to create the type of world in which they themselves can live comfortably, safely and happily.

Self-direction. Psychologically healthier people evince a willingness to co-operate with other human beings, as this will often be in their own best interest and will assist in the survival of the social group. They tend, however, to assume primary responsibility for establishing meaningful personal goals and working to attain these goals; they do not form overly dependent relationships with others or demand support and succour from them.

Tolerance.   According to Ellis, individuals with a greater degree of psychological health will apply a philosophy of tolerance when confronted with conditions or events that conflict with their own basic values, goals and preferences. This means that they will refrain from globally damning themselves or others for unaccept-able and obnoxious behaviour, and that they are willing to put up with conditions that involve discomfort and frustration (without awfulizing about these conditions) when doing so will abet their progress toward desired goals. They tend to practise the ideas embodied in the prayer of Saint Francis insofar as they will work to change undesirable conditions that *can* be changed, and accept (and adapt to as best they can) unfortunate conditions that cannot be changed.

Flexibility.   This criterion refers to the tendencies of psychologi-cally healthier people to be flexible in their thinking, open to change, and unbigoted and pluralistic in their views of other people. They see that it is potentially self-defeating to make invariant, rigid rules for themselves and others, as such rules will most likely lead them into upsets and dysfunctional behaviour.

Acceptance of Uncertainty.   According to Ellis, psychologically healthier individuals tend to acknowledge and accept the reality of living in a world of probability and chance. They recognize that absolute and invariant certainties do not, and probably never will, exist. They are able to see that existence in such a world can often be exciting and interesting, and never has to be regarded as awful. They recognize the benefits of introducing a reasonable amount of order into their lives but do not demand to know exactly what the future will bring.

Commitment to Creative Pursuits.   In Ellis's view, better adjusted individuals see the value in becoming vitally absorbed in some interest or activity outside of themselves. As such, they often develop creative pursuits, as well as some form of major human involvement, and consider these activities so important that they structure a good part of their daily existence around them. They tend, however, not to sacralize these activities. They would not, for example, become dogmatic adherents to the views of a particular religious group or political party.

Scientific Thinking. Ellis holds that people who are relatively free from emotional disturbance will tend to be more objective, rational and scientific in their thinking, as compared with more disturbed individuals. While able to feel deeply and act concertedly, they choose to regulate their emotions and actions by reflecting upon them in an appropriate, not overly self-involved manner. In this way they can evaluate the consequences of their emotions and actions in terms of the degree to which they contribute to the attainment of valued goals. Human beings who practise scientific thinking are willing to revise their hypotheses about self, others and the world when confronted with convincing evidence that their current hypotheses lack validity.

Self-acceptance. Psychologically healthier individuals are able to recognize that as complex human beings, they have both good *and* bad characteristics. Unlike more disturbed individuals, they refrain from trying to globally rate their intrinsic worth (either positively *or* negatively) on the basis of these characteristics. Instead, they choose to accept themselves unconditionally, and attempt to enjoy rather than prove themselves.

Risk-taking. In Ellis's view, emotionally healthier people are more amenable to taking reasonable risks in order to achieve the goals they set for themselves. In this sense they tend to be adventurous but not foolhardy. They tend not to awfulize when confronted with the possibility or the actuality of failure.

Long-range Hedonism. Ellis considers that psychologically healthier people are hedonistic in the sense that they will act in ways that will maximise their pleasure and satisfaction in life, with respect to both the present moment *and* the future. They evince a willingness to endure present pain for long-range gain, and are not obsessed with immediate gratification. Recognizing that they will probably continue to live for quite a few more years, they refrain from making choices and engaging in behaviours (for example, over-eating, smoking) that may significantly jeopardize their long-term health and happiness.

Non-Utopianism. Emotionally healthier people accept that the world, other people and they themselves are imperfect, and that circumstances will probably never be such that they manage to get everything they want and avoid all pain. They refuse to strive unrealistically for total joy, happiness or perfection, or for a complete absence of disturbing (but very human) feelings such as anxiety, depression and anger. Nevertheless, they determine to make the best of the imperfect conditions with which they are inevitably confronted.

Self-responsibility for Own Disturbance. Ellis posits that healthier people are more willing to accept a greater degree of responsibility for their own emotional and behavioural disturbances. They choose not to defensively blame others or social conditions for their problems, and are more likely to take on the effort required to improve their psychological functioning.

Ellis and rational emotive behaviour therapy have sometimes been criticized for emphasizing self-interest and long-range hedonism as criteria for sound psychological health. These criticisms have, however, been largely founded upon misunderstandings of Ellis's use of these terms. Self-interest, for example, has been equated by critics with selfishness. If, however, we define selfishness as 'the ruthless pursuit of one's own goals while cynically disregarding the goals and values of others', then it is certain that Ellis is not advocating that individuals act selfishly. Instead, he is advocating that individuals assume the primary responsibility for acknowledging their own values and working toward their own goals, as opposed to becoming unduly dependent upon others for their satisfaction and happiness. It is also noted that Ellis promotes the concept of social interest as an additional criterion of psychological health, and it is probably safe to say that a philosophy of social interest and a 'selfish' approach to living are mutually exclusive (Ellis, 1967, 1987c; Ellis and Bernard, 1985).

With respect to the criterion of long-range hedonism, critics have sometimes equated this with a slavish devotion to 'the pleasures of the flesh'. Here, they are focusing on the word 'hedonism' and apparently ignoring the qualifying term 'long-range'. Long-range hedonists may indeed be interested in pursuing the 'pleasures of the flesh', but not in a manner that will ultimately prove self-defeating. They are future- as well as present-oriented, and try to make decisions and act in ways that will maximize their enjoyment and satisfaction in life over the long-term. Since they want to live in the type of world that would help them to do so, they would tend not to pursue happiness and pleasure in ways that would harm other individuals or the larger social group.

It is important to note that Ellis (1977c) accords the concept of self-acceptance a place of central importance within his approach to psychotherapy. This emphasis upon helping clients to approach a philosophy of self-acceptance can be viewed as distinctly setting

REBT apart from many other types of therapy and counselling. Numerous other approaches try to help clients to elevate their 'self-esteem' and feelings of 'self-worth', typically by providing them with excessive amounts of warmth and support and by absolving them from responsibility for their emotional disturbance. As a result, individuals treated with these alternative forms of therapy and counselling may become ever more self-pitying and learn to blame others and the world for their problems; their increased self-esteem may be largely contingent upon the ongoing approval and support provided by their therapists. Ellis, however, attempts to teach clients to unconditionally accept themselves as fallible human beings who nonetheless have the capacity to appreciate and enjoy the fact that they are alive. He rejects global person-rating of any sort, as he holds that human beings are too complex and fluid to ever warrant a single, all-encompassing rating. Ellis (1977c), in fact, has referred to self-esteem as representing a form of disturbance, as it connotes a positive overall rating of self. This positive rating of self would have to be based upon some thing or things (such as the approval of others, possession of a positive trait, or good performance in a field of endeavour), and individuals who give themselves a global positive rating in the present may be vulnerable to giving themselves a global negative rating in the future when they fail in some personally meaningful way to live up to their own standards for self-worth.

The final criterion in the list presented above makes reference to assuming responsibility for one's own emotional disturbance. This criterion is particularly important from the REBT perspective, as it is unlikely that individuals who continue to blame their problems on factors external to themselves will experience much success in improving their psychological health. Ellis (1977d), in fact, holds that acknowledging one's own role in creating one's emotional disturbance is fundamental to meaningful change within therapy or counselling. The sections that follow will detail Ellis's views on insights essential to the process of therapeutic change, and will describe the procedures he has created to assist therapy clients in challenging and replacing their irrational beliefs.

Ellis's Perspective on the Process of Therapeutic Change

When individuals first enter psychotherapy or counselling, they may well have certain views on the nature and origin of their emotional problems that will effectively block them from deriving any substantial benefits from treatment. Here we are referring to the very human tendency (fostered by popularized presentations of approaches such as psychoanalysis and behaviour therapy) to ascribe one's psychological difficulties to external factors. For many persons, these factors may include such things as an overly critical spouse, a stress-filled work environment or home life, and a poor upbringing by one's parents. Thus, a good number of novice therapy clients may subscribe to views such as the following: 'Oh, the reason I lack confidence in myself and feel depressed is because my lousy parents criticized me too much and hardly ever praised me. It's really their fault that I'm all screwed up!'

The Three Main Insights of RET

Before significant gains can be made in therapy, it is important for clients to stop blaming conditions and other people for their problems. Ellis (1977d) thus believes that a fundamental task of the rational emotive behaviour therapist is to convey the following three main insights of REBT to clients.

> *Insight no. 1*:   You largely *choose* to disturb yourself about the unpleasant events of your life, although you may be encouraged to do so by external happenings and by social learning. You mainly feel the way you think. When obnoxious and frustrating things happen to you at point A (activating events) you consciously or unconsciously *select* rational beliefs (rBs) that lead you to feel sad and regretful and you also *select* irrational beliefs (iBs) that lead you to feel anxious, depressed and self-hating.
>
> *Insight no. 2*:   No matter how or when you acquired your irrational beliefs and self-sabotaging habits, you now, in the present, *choose* to maintain them – and that is why you are *now* disturbed. Your past history and your present life conditions importantly *affect* you, but they don't *disturb* you. Your present *philosophy* is the main contributor to your *current* disturbance.
>
> *Insight no. 3*:   There is no magical way for you to change your personality and your strong tendencies to needlessly upset yourself. Basic personality change requires persistent *work and practice* – yes, *work and practice* – to enable you to alter your irrational beliefs, your inappropriate feelings and your self-destructive behaviors.
> (Ellis, 1984c: 2)

Implications of REBT's Three Main Insights

It will be apparent to the reader that these three insights put forward by Ellis (1977d, 1984c) give primary responsibility to the client as (a) the agent who creates and adheres to the irrational beliefs that are implicated in the individual's current emotional disturbance and (b) the agent who is capable, largely through his or her own concerted efforts, of rejecting these irrational beliefs and replacing them with more rational, constructive ones. While these tenets may seem to place an unnecessary and unhelpful burden upon the client, they can also be viewed as setting the stage to encourage clients to fully face and deal with their problems. Also, these insights can be regarded as personally liberating for clients: rather than ascribing their psychological difficulties to external factors that may be unmodifiable and beyond their control, they can instead choose to view their problems as being within their power to change. This is in reality a rather optimistic perspective on what clients can hope to gain through their participation in counselling or therapy.

In outlining insight no. 3, Ellis (1984c) strongly makes the point that clients will have to work in a determined and consistent manner in order to alter their dysfunctional beliefs, emotions and behaviours. His long clinical experience has taught him that there is simply no easy and comfortable way to affect meaningful therapeutic change, and he often attempts to convey this teaching to the individuals with whom he works. Ellis's powerful emphasis on 'work and practice' for clients in therapy is another aspect of his approach that sets him apart from the major advocates of other therapeutic schools.

Disputing Irrational Beliefs: A Major Technique for Affecting Therapeutic Change

Ellis (1962; Ellis and Whiteley, 1979) argues in favour of the principal of psychological interactionism, insofar as he acknowledges that beliefs, emotions and behaviours significantly interact and overlap, and in reality cannot be regarded as entities that are clearly distinct from one another. Nevertheless, he focuses most of his therapeutic energies on helping clients to surrender the irrational beliefs that underpin their dysfunctional emotions and behaviours. This is largely because he views basic philosophical change as the most effective route to improved psychological health.

In order to promote basic philosophical change, Ellis teaches his clients to dispute their irrational beliefs. In this context, disputing refers to a process of first identifying and then challenging (through a series of questions) irrational beliefs, with the goal of demonstrating that these beliefs are (a) illogical; (b) distortions of reality; and (c) unhelpful insofar as they contribute to emotional upsets and episodes of self-defeating behaviour. Ellis (1977b) has described three major components to the process of disputing irrational beliefs:

Detecting Irrational Beliefs. This refers to the task of identifying the irrational beliefs in one's thinking that contribute to one's disturbance. With respect to detecting irrational beliefs, Ellis has written the following:

> You first assume, on theoretical grounds, if you follow the RET approach, that when you feel anxious, depressed, self-downing, guilty, hostile, or otherwise emotionally upset, you have some kinds of *shoulds* or *musts* that you keep strongly telling yourself; and you *look for* these absolutes or magical demands. 'What *should* or *must* do I keep telling myself to *create* my disturbance?' you ask yourself. 'Do I have them in my social life? My sex life? My school life? My career? Where?'
>
> Quite quickly, once you get adept at looking for these demands, you will start to find them. Then you can also do the same thing about your other irrational thinking, most notably your *awfulizing* and your *can't-stand-its*, and your damning of yourself and/or others. For whenever you experience distinct emotional problems, you can assume that your irrational beliefs take one or more of four basic forms, all of which appear related to each other: (1) you think that someone or something *should, ought* or *must* be different from the way it actually does exist; (2) you find it *awful, terrible,* or *horrible* when it is this way; (3) you think that you *can't bear, stand* or *tolerate* this person or thing that you concluded *should* not have been as it is; (4) you think that you or some other person (or people) have made or keep making horrible errors and that because you or they must not act the way they clearly do act, you or they deserve nothing good in life, merit *damnation,* and can legitimately receive the label of *louse, rotten person,* or *turd.* (Ellis, 1977b: 9–10)

Debating Irrational Beliefs.   This refers to the process of challenging the validity of the irrational beliefs that were detected and found to be operative in a given instance or type of emotional disturbance. In his own words, Ellis has described this component of the disputing process thus:

> RET largely consists of the use of the logico-empirical method of scientific questioning, challenging, and debating.
>
> You take each of your irrational beliefs that you arrived at during the Detecting process and you ask: 'What evidence supports it? In which way does it have truth – or falseness? What makes it so?
>
> This kind of Debating, of course, really consists of rhetorical questions designed to dispute and to rip up the *false* Belief. For in RET we assume that if you have a dysfunctional behavior or emotional Consequence (C) following the occurrence of some Activating Experience or Event (A), you almost certainly have some kind of Belief (B) that directly sparks this Consequence, and that Belief has irrational elements in it and therefore constitutes an irrational Belief (iB). The scientific method takes any shaky hypothesis, particularly one that leads to poor results, and actively, vigorously disputes it, until it gets surrendered or sustained.
>
> If you find evidence to back this hypothesis, fine: You keep it. If you find evidence against it, or if you don't find any to support it, you give it

up and look for a better one. Your Debating, therefore, involves an internal debate between you and you – between your rational and irrational Beliefs. And the object of the Debating? To destroy, or at least minimize, your iB's. (Ellis, 1977b: 20–1)

Discriminating Irrational Beliefs. This component of disputing refers to distinguishing irrational beliefs from rational beliefs, and reviewing the manner in which the former tend to lead to dysfunctional and the latter to more helpful emotional (and behavioural) consequences. Ellis has described it thus:

> And *Discriminating?* Of what does that consist? It consists of your clearly distinguishing between your wants and your needs, your desires and your demands (or musts), your rational and irrational ideas. The process consists of showing yourself the good as well as the bad points in your behavior; noting the difference between undesirable and 'unbearable' results in your life; showing yourself that hassles do not amount to 'horrors'; differentiating between logical conclusions about your life and non sequiturs; and discerning various other kinds of inconsistencies and contradictions in your thoughts and behaviors as you Debate with yourself the irrational Beliefs that you have Detected . . . in the RET process. (1977b: 21)

Ellis (1979e: 79) has created a technique known by the acronym DIBs (for Disputing Irrational Beliefs) that offers a structured format for disputation by providing a series of questions that clients can apply to their irrational beliefs. These questions are as follows:

1 What irrational belief do I want to dispute and surrender?
2 Can I rationally support this belief?
3 What evidence exists of the falseness of this belief?
4 Does any evidence exist of the truth of this belief?
5 What worst things could *actually* happen to me if I don't get what I think I must (or do get what I think I mustn't)?
6 What good things could I make happen if I don't get what I think I must (or do get what I think I mustn't)?

As will be seen in Chapter 3, DIBs is not the only format available for challenging irrational beliefs. It does, however, help to illustrate the different aspects of the questioning process that Ellis attempts to teach to his clients.

Additional Comments on Disputing and the Process of Therapeutic Change

The sections above detailed the detecting, debating and discriminating components of the disputing process. In order to have a complete understanding of Ellis's views on disputing and the process of therapeutic change, the reader should also be aware that he advocates a multi-modal approach; encourages profound philosophical change; advocates therapeutic homework assignments and distinguishes between intellectual and emotional insight.

A Multi-modal Approach.   Ellis's writings (and audio-recordings of his clinical sessions with clients; see Yankura and Dryden, 1990) reveal that he places a particularly strong focus upon identifying and verbally disputing clients' irrational beliefs. Here, 'verbal disputing' refers to the procedure of helping clients to see the irrational beliefs to which they subscribe and then (through a combination of directive questioning and didactic teaching) showing them why these beliefs are illogical, inconsistent with reality and unhelpful. Despite his focus on verbal disputing, Ellis (1979e, 1985c) is quite strong in advocating that counsellors and therapists adopt a multi-modal approach in assisting clients to surrender their self-defeating personal philosophies. Thus, in his own work with clients, he will utilize (and suggest that clients employ on an independent basis) cognitive, behavioural and emotive techniques. This is because he believes (on the basis of his clinical experience) that individuals will experience greater success in achieving cognitive change if they attack their irrational beliefs in a variety of ways and on a number of different dimensions. It is important to note, however, that the choice of techniques is guided by the rational-emotive theory of psychological disturbance and health. As such, Ellis chooses methods that have the potential to facilitate helpful philosophical changes, and generally avoids using methods that are merely palliative (in terms of only distracting clients from adhering to their usual irrational beliefs) or may inadvertently reinforce irrational thinking (such as therapists providing clients with excessive amounts of warmth and love). Further details on the arsenal of techniques that Ellis advocates in therapy will be provided in Chapter 3.

Profound Philosophical Change.   Whenever feasible, Ellis encourages clients to achieve lasting, profound philosophical change. This would mean that they mainly no longer adhere to their absolutistic beliefs about self, others and the world, but stay primarily with their preferences, wants and desires. Such change has been described by Ellis in the following terms:

> RET especially tries, in most cases, to help bring about an elegant, long-lasting state of improvement whereby clients, first, give up their presenting symptoms (e.g., social anxiety); second, diminish or eliminate other dysfunctional symptoms (e.g., work or sports anxiety); third,

maintain their therapeutic progress; fourth, become less likely, by using RET over the years, to seriously disturb themselves again; fifth, when they occasionally fall back to emotional and behavioral problems use RET again to quickly overcome their recurring or newly created difficulties; and sixth, keep seeking and finding maximally enjoyable, but nondefeating, paths to personal enjoyment. (1991c: 8)

Despite his focus on profound philosophical change, Ellis recognizes that not all individuals in therapy desire or are able to approach this goal. Some clients, for example, seek help for only one or two rather circumscribed problem areas in their lives, and are not really motivated to address the manner in which irrational thinking may impact upon other aspects of their functioning. Also, intellectually limited or very unsophisticated clients may lack the personal resources that would allow them to understand and then work toward the type of deep-seated, pervasive philosophical modifications that REBT can facilitate in some cases. As such, Ellis incorporates a good deal of flexibility into his therapeutic work. He accepts the fact that some individuals may terminate treatment after experiencing relief from their original presenting problem(s), and recognizes that limited individuals are likely to make more modest gains.

Therapeutic Homework Assignments. Ellis (1980b) is concerned with promoting efficiency in psychotherapy and counselling, and also with discouraging clients from becoming dependent upon their therapists. Homework assignments represent a vehicle for addressing both of these concerns. First, they help to promote efficient therapy by extending 'treatment time' beyond the traditional therapeutic hour (or half-hour, as is often the case in Ellis's practice). Clients who agree to undertake homework assignments continue working on their problem areas (and at modifying the irrational beliefs that underpin them) between therapy sessions. When efforts at change are extended out into the 'real world' in this fashion, therapeutic gains may be experienced more quickly. Second, homework assignments encourage clients to make independent efforts at changing themselves, as the therapist very probably will not be present at the time that such assignments are enacted. When clients are able to attribute therapeutic changes to their own (as opposed to their therapists') efforts, they may then be less likely to form overly dependent relationships with their therapists and more likely to believe in their own personal efficacy. Ellis, of course, believes that it is beneficial for clients to take on homework assignments that encourage them to dispute their irrational beliefs through a variety of means.

Two Types of Insight. Ellis has written of the distinction between *intellectual insight* and *emotional insight* as it relates to the therapeutic change process within rational emotive behaviour therapy:

> people who have intellectual insight see how they create their own disturbances and what they can do about uncreating them, but tend to see these things lightly, occasionally, and weakly; those who have emotional insight see the same things intensely, often, and strongly. Sometimes, more to the point, people with emotional insight normally work very hard, very often, and very powerfully at giving up their self-defeating Beliefs and acting against them, while people with intellectual insight do this kind of work mildly, seldom, and weakly. (1979d: 87)

To further clarify the difference between intellectual and emotional insight, Hauck (personal communication to Dryden, 1989) has suggested that the former refers to *understanding*, while the latter refers to *conviction*. Clients who have attained intellectual insight *understand* the rational-emotive position on the relationship between their irrational beliefs and the self-defeating emotional and behavioural consequences they experience. Clients who have acquired emotional insight have achieved a degree of conviction about this premise that leads them to frequently act upon it (and thus further their conviction in it). Compared to individuals with intellectual insight, individuals with emotional insight subscribe more strongly to their rational beliefs than to their irrational ones. An important task of rational emotive behaviour therapists is therefore to help clients to move from intellectual insight to emotional insight. This movement can be facilitated with the variety of cognitive, emotive, and behavioural techniques to be described in Chapter 3.

Ellis's Views on the Possibility of Attaining Meaningful Philosophical Change

As noted earlier, Ellis (1976a, 1979a) has advanced the hypothesis that human beings are biologically predisposed to engage in irrational thinking. Even individuals raised in the most supportive and reasonable environments will often tend to create all sorts of absolutistic, disturbance-producing shoulds, musts and oughts to which they rigidly subscribe. Ellis takes the position that the biologically based tendency to construct and then adhere to irrational beliefs can be quite difficult to modify, and that, for most people, it probably cannot be totally eradicated.

Ellis's writings on this issue indicate that he views human beings as having varying capacities to approach (through a psychotherapeutic experience or other means) a complete, pervasive and enduring rational philosophy of life. Some individuals, being less predisposed to engage in irrational thinking, may naturally be less prone to disturb themselves about the unfortunate events or circumstances with which they may be faced – and when they do experience an upset, they may be able to effectively and swiftly deal with it by examining and modifying their beliefs. For the majority of individuals, however, merely approaching the goal of a rational philosophy will require a great amount of self-discipline and prolonged effort. This state of affairs can be viewed as representing a catch-22 situation for psychotherapy and counselling clients, as many of them enter treatment with what Ellis would describe as abysmally low frustration tolerance. Even for clients who are able to maintain an above-average level of effort, periodic backsliding to irrational thinking (and concomitant upsets) is regarded as almost inevitable (Ellis, 1984c, 1985c).

In addition to low frustration tolerance, Ellis (1983d, 1987a) has identified the following factors as representing obstacles to helping individuals replace their self-defeating philosophies with more functional ones.

1 *Demands for quick relief*: Most people tend to be attracted to methods that promise quick and easy relief from emotional distress. These methods, however, are likely to afford only temporary relief, and may distract individuals from working to approach the types of basic philosophical changes that are more likely to provide meaningful benefits.

2 *Changing circumstances*: Unfortunate conditions (that is, negative activating events) about which individuals upset themselves may serve as the initial impetus for some of them to seek therapy. These activating events may, however, fortuitously change for the better, discouraging some clients from staying in treatment and pursuing meaningful philosophical change. Many people terminate treatment when some stressor in their lives is no longer impacting upon them.

3 *Secondary disturbances*: As described earlier, human beings create their primary emotional disturbances and *then* often disturb themselves about these primary problems. Thus, they create a secondary level of disturbance. This secondary level of disturbance increases the complexity and difficulty involved in becoming 'symptom free'.

4 *Subtle irrationalities*: Many individuals – particularly those who have a greater tendency to disturb themselves – hold both

blatant and subtle irrational beliefs. Subtle irrational beliefs are more difficult for both client and therapist to detect, and hence more difficult to challenge.

5 *Reinforcement of irrational thinking*: The emotional and behavioural effects of adhering to certain irrational beliefs can sometimes lead to reinforcing consequences, which may serve to augment the degree to which an individual subscribes to these beliefs. To cite an example, the irrational belief, 'Others *must* treat me with consideration', can lead to anger and aggressive behaviour when a person subscribing to this belief is treated inconsiderately by others. A display of anger and aggressive verbal behaviour may in some instances result in a favourable modification in the way one is treated by these others. Anger and aggressive behaviour are thus reinforced, and the belief that underpins them is strengthened.

6 *Hopelessness*: When individuals have experienced particular emotional and behavioural problems over and over again for a long period of time, they may incorrectly conclude that these difficulties are completely unmodifiable. This conclusion would probably tend to discourage them from entering or sticking with therapy.

7 *Other cognitive factors*:   Ellis (1985c, 1987a) has noted that ignorance, limited intellectual potential, limited perceptiveness, and defensiveness can all also represent significant obstacles to approaching meaningful philosophical change.

Ellis (Weinrach and Ellis, 1980) has commented upon his own difficulties in minimizing particular sorts of emotional upsets. As noted in Chapter 1, while he reports that he almost never causes himself to experience anxiety or depression, he acknowledges that he has had to work at overcoming a tendency towards anger and irritability. While he still sometimes experiences these emotions, he makes concerted efforts (by detecting and debating his own irrational beliefs) to help himself quickly change them to a feeling of mere annoyance. He reminds himself – quite strongly – that no matter how poorly another person may behave, they never rate as a totally damnable, rotten human being.

Despite the large number of factors which can increase the difficulty of approaching a truly rational philosophy of life, Ellis (1987a) has described himself as optimistic with respect to the capacity of human beings to improve their mental health. While he believes that humans are biologically predisposed to think irrationally, he also views them as possessing considerable self-actualizing tendencies (Ellis, 1962, 1987a, 1991d; Dryden and Ellis,

1986). In addition, he sees various ways in which psychotherapy in general and REBT in particular can be refined (Ellis, 1982, 1983d, 1985c, 1987c; Bernard, 1986). Finally, Ellis anticipates a day when guidelines for rational living will routinely be conveyed in schools and other important societal institutions, as well as effectively conveyed through the mass media. He holds the opinion that early and consistent exposure to this material may well help humankind to counter its innate tendencies to think, emote and act irrationally.

Note

1 Healthy and unhealthy negative emotions used to be known as appropriate and inappropriate negative emotions. However, the terms 'appropriate' and 'inappropriate' are ambiguous and give rise to a number of misunderstandings. Hence the change of terms.

3

Major Contributions to Practice

The central theme of RET is that humans are uniquely rational, as well as uniquely irrational, animals; that their emotional or psychological disturbances are largely a result of their thinking illogically or irrationally, and that they can rid themselves of most of their emotional or mental unhappiness, ineffectuality, and disturbance if they learn to maximize their rational and minimize their irrational thinking.

(Ellis, 1962: 36)

Overview

In presenting Ellis's major contributions to the practice of therapy and counselling, we have divided this chapter into five major sections. The first section deals with Ellis's views on what constitutes sound treatment, and also presents his opinions on treatments and methods that he views as being inefficient, ineffective and potentially harmful to clients. The second section details his approach to client assessment within therapy. As will be seen, his views and practice with regard to assessment differ from mainstream practice in some important ways. The third section deals with Ellis's contributions to intervention procedures, and describes the various cognitive, behavioural and emotive methods that he employs in his work with clients. Section four presents Ellis's approach to resistance within counselling and psychotherapy, while the final section outlines his thoughts on particular irrational beliefs to which mental health practitioners may sometimes subscribe while practising therapy.

Ellis's Views on Sound Treatment

Throughout most of his professional career, dating back to his early dissatisfaction with the psychoanalytic approach to therapy, Ellis has maintained a strong interest in promoting effective and efficient treatment of clients' problems. In the following sections we detail

his thoughts on the characteristics of sound therapy and counselling, the characteristics of effective rational emotive behaviour
therapists, and the therapeutic conditions that such therapists strive
to establish in their work with clients.

The Characteristics of Efficient Therapy

Ellis (1980b) has noted that psychotherapy outcome research is
often focused upon testing the *effectiveness* of a given form of
treatment. Studies are conducted in which subjects are divided into
groups receiving (a) the treatment in question, (b) an alternative
form of treatment and/or (c) a placebo treatment or no treatment at
all. When the treatment under scrutiny results in significant gains
for the 'treatment' group, it is said to possess some degree of
effectiveness. Ellis (1980b: 414) has observed, however, that
therapy researchers rarely test the *efficiency* of treatments 'to
determine, on a cost-benefit basis, how much time and effort is
normally spent by therapists and clients to achieve "effective"
results . . .'. In addressing this issue, he has advanced a number of
criteria for therapy that is efficient as well as effective.

Brevity. Ellis (1980b) notes that efficient psychotherapy helps
clients to make improvements in their problem areas in a relatively
brief period of time. This has obvious advantages for clients with
respect to minimizing the amount of time and money that they have
to expend on treatment, and also benefits governmental agencies
and insurance companies that subsidize, in one form or another,
mental health care. By taking an active-directive stance and
pursuing a psychoeducational approach to treatment, Ellis hopes to
be able to quickly show his clients the origins and solutions to their
emotional and behavioural problems.

Depth-centredness. Efficient therapy tends to be depth-centred,
but not necessarily in the sense espoused by the psychoanalytic
approach. In referring to depth-centredness, Ellis (1980b) advocates
that therapists assist clients in (a) identifying their fundamental
disturbance-creating beliefs, and (b) surrendering these beliefs and
replacing them with a more rational philosophy. This approach to
depth-centredness can help clients to obtain a clearer view of how
they disturb themselves, learn how to lead a more fulfilling
existence and obtain a more general understanding of human
nature that may have a beneficial impact on many aspects of living.

Pervasiveness. Ellis (1980b: 415) defines pervasiveness in psychotherapy as 'the therapist's helping clients to deal with many of their

problems, and in a sense their whole lives, rather than with a few presenting symptoms'. In REBT, this can mean showing clients the core irrational beliefs to which they subscribe, and teaching them how these beliefs may be implicated not only in their original presenting complaints, but also in other problematic areas of their lives as well. Ellis notes that

> pervasiveness in psychotherapy has distinct benefits: (1) It shows clients how they can easily create several symptoms from the same underlying attitudes and feelings and how, by changing these attitudes, they can deal with or eliminate more than one or two presenting symptoms, (2) it helps them to understand and relate better to other people, (3) it may enable them, especially if they learn to apply a form of treatment like REBT, how to deal therapeutically with their close associates. (1980b: 415)

Extensiveness.   Ellis (1980b) distinguishes between treatment that is *intensive* and treatment that is *extensive*. Intensive therapy assists clients in dealing with problems such as severe emotional pain, inhibition, panic and horror. Extensive therapy, on the other hand, not only helps clients to minimize their severely dysfunctional negative feelings, but also helps them to maximize their potential for a satisfying, happy existence. Thus, in Ellis's (1980b) view, efficient psychotherapy would tend to employ self-actualizing procedures as well as the means for alleviating emotional disturbance. In his work with clients, Ellis (1991d) can be quite explicit in teaching them how they might explore and approach self-actualization.

Thoroughgoingness.   Noting that cognition, emotion, and behaviour are aspects of human functioning that significantly interact and overlap, Ellis (1980b) advocates an approach to therapy that is multi-modal in nature. This means that therapists will selectively employ a variety of procedures and techniques to help clients attain relief from their psychological problems. Most clients will probably achieve better results in therapy if their problems are thoroughly addressed on a number of different levels. Ellis operates from a rational-emotive theoretical base, but may judiciously employ techniques and strategies derived from other approaches in attempting to help clients make meaningful philosophical changes.

Maintenance of Therapeutic Progress.   In discussing this aspect of efficient treatment, Ellis describes several limitations of 'symptom removal' approaches to psychotherapy:

(1) When a given symptom is removed or ameliorated, another may easily spring up later – not necessarily because of symptom substitution but as a derivative of the same basic self-defeating philosophy with which clients create their original symptoms. (2) Many clients feel so relieved by the temporary or partial removal of a painful symptom (e.g., depression) that they leave the core of it (or its close relatives) still standing. (3) Most clients have some degree of low frustration tolerance and therefore will welcome palliative procedures (e.g., tranquilizers or relaxation methods) to quickly alleviate their worst symptoms rather than working at more elegant philosophical changes that will result in more permanent changes. (1980b:416)

Efficient therapy, according to Ellis, does not strive merely for symptom removal; it seeks to achieve more lasting therapeutic gain. It is his hope that by the end of treatment clients will feel significantly better, and will *continue* improving (by using the REBT self-help techniques they learned in therapy) for a considerable period of time after therapy termination.

A Preventative Focus. Related to the issue of maintaining therapeutic progress, Ellis has written that efficient psychotherapy also teaches clients 'how to ward off future emotion ills and . . . keep themselves from returning to their old disturbed pathways' (1980b: 416). Psychotherapy that includes this preventative quality is clearly more cost-effective, as it obviates the need for a later return to treatment. Ellis encourages clients to continue practising the REBT self-help procedures they've learned after their formal therapy has ended, as this will increase their chances of internalizing the sort of rational philosophy that will make them less vulnerable to future emotional upsets.

Additional Characteristics of Sound Treatment

In addition to the criteria for efficient psychotherapy detailed above, Ellis has identified a number of other elements that, in his view, would tend to be characteristic of effective treatment.

A Philosophical Focus. With respect to this criterion, Ellis has noted the following:

RET is not only cognitive but also highly philosophical and I probably never would have created it in 1955 had I not been convinced for about 20 years before that time that, if people had a truly sound philosophy, they could ward off practically all neurotic thinking, feeling, and behaving and could arrange their lives so that they would rarely, if ever, be self-defeating and antisocial. (1991c: 8–9)

Ellis (1988a) contends that therapies that promote profound

philosophic change are likely to help clients attain positive and enduring changes in their emotional and behavioural functioning. In his view, emotional and behavioural change are frequent concomitants of philosophic change because 'profound philosophic changes are likely to be comprised of fairly hot cognitions that include *strong* feeling and action tendencies' (Ellis, 1988a: 398).

Helping Clients to Get Better Rather than Merely Feel Better. In Ellis's (1972b) view, treatment approaches can in a sense be classified as to whether they truly help clients to *get* better, or merely to *feel* better in a rather temporary fashion. There are many ways for therapists to help their clients to feel better – for example, by teaching them relaxation techniques, providing them with reassurances and offering them warmth and support – but the majority of these methods are probably unlikely, in most cases, to help clients to become less disturbed and better able to cope with life's vicissitudes in any meaningful way. According to Ellis, REBT attempts to help clients to genuinely get better by showing them quite specifically how they disturb themselves, and then providing them with the means to minimize their disturbance.

Utilization of Implosive Homework Assignments. Ellis (1982, 1983a) has written of the risks that may be inherent in therapeutic 'gradualism'. By gradualism, he means therapeutic strategies and techniques that encourage clients to approach feared stimuli and other emotionally problematic situations in a gradual, step-wise progression (for example, systematic desensitization). In his view, such methods may inadvertently serve to reinforce certain irrational beliefs that clients may hold (this issue will receive further discussion in the section below on 'Potentially Harmful Methods'). Ellis promotes the use of an implosive or flooding approach to homework assignments in therapy, as he explains in the following excerpt:

> Most therapies, and especially cognitive-behavioral therapy, use gradual homework assignments, such as encouraging clients to do imaginal or *in vivo* desensitization once or a few times a week (Wolpe, 1983). RET often does this, too. But I often encourage suitable (and sometimes even difficult) clients to do the homework implosively, if feasible, 10 or 20 times a day. Thus, I may induce cigarette addicts to make a list of the disadvantages of smoking and to forcefully go over this list 10 or 20 times every day. Or I persuade elevator phobics to take elevator rides 25 times every day while they are also telling themselves, 'I don't *need* a guarantee that this elevator won't fall, but there is very little probability that it will. I *can* stand the discomfort of riding in elevators, and if I do so, I will soon feel comfortable!' I find that, when this kind of

homework is done, therapy is frequently briefer and more effective. (1991c: 3)

In Ellis's view therapy may be briefer and more effective when implosive methods are utilized because such methods provide clients with opportunities to directly confront, challenge and replace their upset-producing irrational beliefs. Such efforts on the part of clients are more likely to lead to the profound philosophic changes advocated in REBT.

Applying Force and Energy in Disputing Irrational Beliefs. Clients often adhere to their irrational beliefs with formidable tenacity, even after they see that these beliefs significantly contribute to emotional and dysfunctional behaviours. Thus, Ellis (1979d, 1985c, 1991c) has often made the case that it is advisable for therapists to show their clients (through modelling and direct teaching) how to attack their irrational beliefs with considerable force and energy. Clients who only engage in mild and occasional disputing may attain *intellectual* insight, but may fail to achieve *emotional* insight (see the discussion on these two types of insight in Chapter 2). As a result, they may lightly acknowledge the validity of a rational belief that has relevance to their particular problem area, but more strongly hold to their disturbance-creating irrational belief. In order to remedy this situation they may, for example, engage in frequent practice of powerful rational self-statements such as the following: 'I may *want* the approval and approbation of my colleagues at work, but there's no damned reason why I *have to* have it! FUCK IT! I can damn well live and be happy without it!' Note that this self-statement incorporates profanity, which for some individuals can be an effective means of increasing the impact of a rational message.

The Characteristics of Effective Rational Emotive Behaviour Therapists

In addition to writing about the elements that characterize sound treatment, Ellis (1978, 1987c) has also outlined what he views to be the characteristics of effective rational emotive behaviour therapists.

1 They enjoy being active and directive in their work with clients. This characteristic is important since Ellis advocates conducting REBT in a strong active-directive manner. In particular, he maintains that clients will generally experience more success in surrendering their irrational beliefs when these are disputed in an energetic and forceful manner (Ellis, 1979d). Through their in-session behaviour, therapists can model the application of

force and energy to the disputing process such that clients can learn to do this on an independent basis.

2   They tend to be devoted to philosophy, science, logic and empiricism. REBT is a non-mystical, anti-absolutist approach to therapy that seeks to teach clients to become better scientists with respect to overcoming their emotional and behavioural problems. As such, its effective practitioners are comfortable with and interested in the application of logic and the scientific method to the process of resolving psychological disturbance. REBT also has a strong philosophical focus, and effective rational emotive behaviour therapists are philosophically inclined and interested in helping their clients to develop a more helpful philosophy of living.

3   Since REBT offers a fairly structured approach to helping clients with their problems, effective rational emotive behaviour therapists are usually comfortable with structure.

4   Nevertheless, they recognize that circumstances may arise wherein a very structured approach to therapy is not feasible (as with clients who tend to have difficulty staying on one topic for any length of time despite the therapist's attempts to help them do so). When confronted by such circumstances, effective rational emotive behaviour therapists are able to exercise flexibility and modify their approach so that their clients will be able to derive maximum benefits from their treatment.

5   In a related vein, they are comfortable with experimentation and take calculated risks in their therapeutic work. While well-informed about the theory and practice of REBT, they adopt a multi-modal approach to treatment and may utilize methods derived from alternative therapies in the service of helping clients to surrender and replace their upset-producing philosophies.

6   As REBT can be viewed as a psychoeducational approach to treatment, effective rational emotive behaviour therapists will tend to have good teaching and communication skills. They are comfortable with the role of 'therapist as teacher', and with providing the sort of active prompting that clients often require if they are to follow through on their therapeutic homework assignments.

7   Effective rational emotive behaviour therapists possess a good sense of humour which they are able to utilize in a manner that benefits clients and facilitates the treatment process. They are able to help clients see the often silly, fallacious nature of their irrational beliefs (in a way that doesn't lead clients to conclude that they are being ridiculed, or to engage in negative self-rating

because they hold such beliefs), and rarely take themselves or their work as therapists *over*-seriously (such that they would not tend to upset themselves about their own personal limitations or the limitations of psychotherapy in general).

8 Importantly, effective practitioners of REBT tend to have high levels of unconditional self-acceptance and frustration tolerance. With regard to unconditional self-acceptance, they do not base their personal worth upon the degree to which their clients improve, nor upon how much their clients appear to approve of them and view them as good therapists. This facilitates their ability to be active-directive within therapy and to be appropriately confrontational with clients in order to show them how they create and maintain their own disturbance. In addition, since they would tend not to rate themselves as failures if they made a mistake within therapy, effective rational emotive behaviour therapists are better able to engage in calculated risk-taking when confronted with therapeutic impasses. With respect to high frustration tolerance, effective REBT therapists do not unduly upset themselves about some of the difficulties inherent in their field of endeavour. Thus, they subscribe to a philosophy that they *can stand* such things as slow client progress, broken appointments, non-compliance with homework assignments, etc. By subscribing to philosophies of unconditional self-acceptance and high frustration tolerance, therapists can be important role models for clients.

To date, the issue of identifying the characteristics of effective REBT therapists has not been studied systematically. The list of characteristics presented here is based upon Ellis's own experience as a practising therapist and supervisor of therapy trainees. Ellis (1978, 1987c) recognizes that not all REBT practitioners have all of these characteristics, and notes that some practitioners appear to modify their implementation of REBT so that it is in accord with their own personality traits. Thus, some therapists tend to practise REBT in a slow-moving, passive manner; do little disputing; and focus therapy on the relationship between themselves and their clients. According to his various writings on this issue, however, it is likely that Ellis would regard this sort of therapeutic style as being less effective and efficient for many clients.

Therapeutic Conditions for Effective Treatment

In addition to outlining his views on the characteristics of effective practitioners of rational emotive behaviour therapy, Ellis has also provided guidelines in his writings concerning the types of therapeutic conditions most likely to contribute to effective treatment. Therapists possessing the characteristics described above would generally tend to try and establish most of these conditions in their work with clients.

Unconditional Acceptance. Ellis (1965b, 1975) encourages therapists to directly teach their clients to become more self-accepting. In addition, he advocates that therapists themselves provide clients with unconditional acceptance within sessions as a less direct means of helping them to approach this aspect of psychological health. This means that therapists refrain from globally rating their clients as bad or worthless individuals, even when they act obnoxiously during therapy or describe anti-social acts they have committed. Rational emotive behaviour therapists deal with such things in a matter-of-fact, non-judgemental fashion, and do not dogmatically insist that their clients *should* behave in certain ways. By establishing an atmosphere of unconditional acceptance, Ellis hopes that clients will be encouraged to accept *themselves* as fallible human beings who engage in both 'good' and 'bad' acts, but who are never *essentially* bad or good. Ellis (1973a) does, however, recommend that therapists comment on aspects of client behaviour which appear to be potentially self-defeating or that seem to impact negatively upon other people (including the therapist). Such feedback is provided in order to help clients modify behaviour patterns that are likely to result in negative consequences, and is intended to help clients to critically examine and rate their acts without rating their 'self'.

Use of Humour. Ellis (1977a, 1987d) believes that *overseriousness* is a major factor involved in most forms of emotional disturbance. In his view, this overseriousness results when individuals apply absolutist, rigid demands (that is, irrational beliefs) to themselves, others and conditions in the world around them. As such, Ellis advocates the use of humorous interventions within therapy sessions as a means for helping clients to overcome their upsets. More specifically, these interventions are targeted at helping clients to see the absurd and illogical aspects of their irrational beliefs. Ellis (1977a), however, cautions therapists to utilize humour in an appropriate fashion that is likely to benefit clients. Thus, while humorous interventions may be used to highlight the fatuous nature of clients' irrational beliefs, they should not be used to poke fun at clients themselves. In addition, Ellis (1984b) strongly advises therapists to refrain from unethically indulging themselves – by over-using humorous or other sorts of interventions – in order to enjoy therapy sessions at their clients' expense. Ellis has noted that when properly used, humour within therapy sessions can serve as:

1 a novel teaching device;
2 a means to help clients view their problems more objectively without rating themselves negatively;
3 a means to temporarily distract clients from subscribing to their disturbance-producing thoughts (such that they may be better able to focus on challenging these thoughts);
4 a means to demonstrate the B–C connection (by showing clients that their improved mood after a humorous intervention can be attributed to changes in their way of thinking about themselves and their life conditions);
5 a vehicle for rapport-building.

Ellis employs several types of humorous interventions in his work with clients, including the use of rational humorous slogans (for example, 'Shouldhood leads to shithood!'), shame-attacking exercises and the highlighting of ironies and contradictions in clients' thinking. For a more detailed discussion of Ellis's use of humorous interventions, the reader is referred to our book, *Doing RET: Albert Ellis in Action* (Yankura and Dryden, 1990).

Therapist as Teacher. In describing his activities with clients during therapy sessions, Ellis (1973b: 15) has noted that 'My main activity, most of the time, consists of involved, concerned, vigorous *teaching*'. Ellis (1978, 1987c) recognizes the value of therapists possessing good teaching and communication skills (see the earlier discussion on the characteristics of effective rational emotive behaviour therapists), and encourages REBT practitioners to adopt the role of authoritative (as opposed to authoritarian) teacher. In implementing this role in his own therapy practice, Ellis attempts to quickly show clients the ABC's of their emotional problems and the means to resolve these problems through the process of disputing. He espouses the use of therapeutic homework assignments as a means for carrying the work of therapy outside of the consultation room, and regularly suggests psychoeducational materials (such as self-help books and audiotapes) that clients may use to hasten and deepen their treatment (Ellis, 1991c).

Avoidance of Excessive Therapist Warmth. Ellis (1967) strongly supports the notion of providing therapy clients with unconditional acceptance, but cautions against therapists offering excessive amounts of warmth to these individuals. With respect to this issue, he has offered the following statement to therapists:

I tried Ferenczi's method (1952) of giving clients considerable warmth and support in the early 1950s and found that they loved it, wanted *more* sessions per week, stayed longer in therapy, and sometimes collaborated more with the therapy procedures. But a great many of them became more (instead of less) dependent on me, increased their dire needs for love and their low frustration tolerance, and became more instead of less disturbed. So for a quick and elegant use of RET, I advise great caution in giving considerable warmth except to a few special (usually borderline and psychotic) clients. Empathic listening and reflective feedback to virtually all clients is fine, but watch your oozing warmth! (Ellis, 1991c: 6)

Ellis (1977e, 1982) has specified two particular risks faced by therapists who rely on conveying excessive warmth and support to their clients. The first risk is that undue amounts of therapist warmth and support may inadvertently reinforce clients' irrational needs for love and approval. Such clients may appear to improve in therapy, but their improvement may actually be a by-product of the fact that they are getting (from their therapist) the love and approval that they believe they *must* have. The second risk relates to inadvertently reinforcing clients' philosophies of low frustration tolerance. This can occur when overly warm therapists refrain from actively encouraging (and when appropriate, strongly pushing) their clients to undertake uncomfortable homework assignments. Therapists who give priority to maintaining a warm relationship with their clients may also avoid confronting them with evidence that they are 'goofing off' (that is, investing little time or energy) with respect to approaching their goals for therapy.

While Ellis has been quite explicit in outlining the potential dangers of excessive therapist warmth, it is important to note that he is not dogmatic in his positions on this issue. The quote cited earlier indicates his recognition that under particular conditions with certain types of clients (for example, with very depressed and emotionally vulnerable individuals) displays of warmth may be therapeutically appropriate for restricted periods of time.

Therapeutic Approaches Regarded by Ellis as Inefficient, Ineffective or Potentially Harmful

The preceding sections have outlined Ellis's thinking on the characteristics of efficient and effective psychotherapy. Ellis has also written extensively on therapeutic approaches that he regards as being less helpful, and in some cases actually harmful, to clients. By reviewing his positions on methods that he deems to be inefficient or potentially harmful, the reader can gain further insights as to his views on sound treatment.

Inefficient and Ineffective Methods

Therapeutic approaches that shift the focus of therapy away from helping clients to identify, challenge and replace their disturbance-producing irrational beliefs are regarded by Ellis as being generally *ineffective*. Techniques that require inordinate amounts of therapy time and large investments of clients' financial resources are viewed as being *inefficient*. Thus, Ellis tends to avoid using things such as dream analysis, detailed exploration of clients' histories, skills training approaches (without concomitant cognitive restructuring) and 'distraction' methods (such as meditation and progressive muscle relaxation) when used mainly by themselves in his clinical practice.

With respect to dream analysis, it is noted that Ellis once wrote a regular column for *Penthouse* magazine in which he provided rational-emotive interpretations of readers' dreams. During his actual therapy sessions, however, Ellis will rarely initiate dream interpretation. When a client presents him with dream material during a session that he or she wishes to examine, Ellis will typically shift the focus of discussion away from the dream's content to consideration of themes that may relate to problems with which the client is currently dealing. Thus, with an individual who tends to make herself feel guilty over self-perceived errors, Ellis may attempt to find 'guilt themes' within any dreams that she may present. He would bring these themes to her attention, and then focus in on helping her to see and alter her guilt-producing philosophy.

Ellis eschews a detailed exploration of clients' past histories and childhood experiences, such as might be pursued in psychoanalytic approaches to therapy. In his view, such exploration will 'lead [clients] up the garden path to scores, sometimes hundreds, of wasted sessions' (1982: 18). He has noted that an overemphasis upon exploration of the past may also hold the following disadvantages for clients:

> [It will] (a) sidetrack them from working hard to change themselves today; (b) provide them with the cop-out of blaming their parents or their society and thereby refusing to take responsibility for their own feelings; (c) help justify the whining, wailing, and sitting on their asses which is almost always the main core of their past and present disturbances; (d) help them get even more hung up than they naturally are on the so-called horror of what was unfairly done to them and thus to get neurotically obsessed more than ever on the past, the past, the

past; (e) encourage them to keep making the major error of wrongly attributing emotional upsets to the events immediately preceding these upsets instead of to their own *view of* and their own *choice of reacting to* such events. (Ellis, 1982: 18)

While Ellis is opposed to detailed exploration of the past on the grounds that it is therapeutically unhelpful, he *will* obtain enough background material on clients (through in-session interviews and review of a biographical form that clients complete) to allow him to begin formulating hypotheses concerning severity of disturbance and the nature of operative irrational beliefs.

Ellis (1982, 1986a, 1991c) also avoids placing an overemphasis upon skills training approaches in his clinical work. In his view, keeping therapy focused mainly on remedying clients' skill deficits (as in social skills and assertiveness training approaches to treatment) may represent another way of sidetracking clients from the important work of identifying and challenging their irrational beliefs. Ellis (1991c: 7) notes that people generally enter therapy with two main sorts of problems: '(1) practical problems of how to get more of what they want and less of what they don't want in life and (2) emotional-behavioral problems *about* their practical problems'. Skills training may help clients to solve their practical problems to some degree, but it may leave untouched the disturbance-producing beliefs that resulted in their emotional-behavioural problems. Thus, clients remain vulnerable to future upsets when their (still operative) irrational beliefs are triggered by new activating events. Ellis will assist clients in strengthening skills areas in which they are weak, but he prefers to de-emphasize this aspect of his therapeutic work until he sees that they are working to give up their irrational beliefs.

Ellis's position regarding what he labels 'distraction' methods is essentially similar to his view on skills training approaches. As noted earlier, distraction methods (according to Ellis's classification) include such things as various approaches to meditation and relaxation training (Ellis, 1982, 1984e). He has written:

> these methods often divert feelings of anxiety, depression, hostility, and self-pity quite effectively but they rarely change the underlying *must*urbatory philosophies that largely create disturbances; and shortly after they have been 'effectively' employed, this disturbance usually returns full blast. (Ellis, 1982: 21)

Thus, clients who over-rely on distraction methods again leave themselves vulnerable to continued upsets. Ellis acknowledges, however, that these methods may in some cases be used in conjunction with disputing techniques to yield some philosophic chang^e (Ellis and Dryden, 1990). As an example, an anxious client may employ a distraction method (such as some variant of a relaxation induction) as a means for temporarily interrupting her anxiety in order to facilitate cognitive disputing.

Potentially Harmful Methods
Within the fields of psychotherapy and medicine, it is recognized that efforts at treatment may sometimes (a) exacerbate already existing symptoms and/or (b) instigate entirely new symptoms. The term *iatrogenesis* is used to describe the creation of additional problems or complications resulting from treatment by a health practitioner. In reviewing Ellis's writings on alternative approaches and techniques within psychotherapy, it appears that he views iatrogenic symptoms as largely being the result of procedures that tend to strengthen clients' irrational beliefs (Ellis, 1982; Ellis and Yeager, 1989). Such procedures will thus lead individuals to become more (instead of less) irrational in their thinking, such that their vulnerability to significant disturbances of emotion and behaviour may be increased. The following list, although not exhaustive, illustrates Ellis's views on the manner in which several currently practised methods may reinforce clients' irrational philosophies:

Approaches which Emphasize Providing Warmth and Love to Clients. These approaches may encourage clients to become dependent upon their therapists and, as noted in the earlier discussion, may reinforce the irrational belief that it is absolutely essential to have the approval of significant others (Ellis, 1982; Dryden and Ellis, 1985).

Catharsis and Abreaction Techniques. These techniques are used with limitations within REBT, as clients are encouraged to fully acknowledge and discuss their feelings about the problematic activating events in their lives (Ellis, 1979e). However, some alternative approaches to treatment (such as primal and Gestalt therapy) place a heavy emphasis upon abreaction and catharsis, particularly with respect to clients releasing 'pent up' feelings of hostility. This emphasis is probably due in part to the view that suppressed emotion is one of the main causes of emotional disturbance. Ellis (1979e, 1982) largely rejects this view, and notes that experimental research in related areas suggests that unbridled ventilation of hostile feelings is more likely to exacerbate than reduce them. He believes that this is due to the fact that when people express their angry feelings without questioning whether these feelings are rational or helpful, they probably tend to re-indoctrinate themselves with their anger-creating ideas. In essence, they are *practising* the irrational beliefs underlying their angry feelings such that they are likely to subscribe ever more strongly to these beliefs.

Gradual Desensitization Techniques. As noted earlier, Ellis is opposed to therapeutic 'gradualism'. Thus, although certain behaviour therapy techniques such as systematic desensitization have demonstrated utility in countering particular types of neurotic symptoms, they may serve to reinforce clients' irrational ideas that (a) it is *awful* to experience emotional discomfort and (b) therapy *should* proceed in a relatively easy, painless fashion (Ellis, 1982, 1983a, 1985c). Ellis (1979b, 1980a, 1990a) regards implosive methods as being potentially more effective and efficient, and as representing a means for countering the discomfort anxiety that clients may experience in relation to their emotional pain and the therapeutic change process.

Approaches which Teach Clients to Depend upon a Higher Power. Some transpersonal approaches to psychotherapy and certain self-help organizations (such as Alcoholics Anonymous, with its twelve-step programme) encourage individuals to utilize the power of a being or a force greater than themselves to overcome personal problems. This can serve to reinforce the irrational belief that 'One *must* have a force or deity upon whom one can depend, as it is impossible to change and improve through one's own efforts' (Ellis, 1985a).

The reader should now be familiar with Ellis's views on what does and what does not constitute sound treatment of emotional and behavioural problems. It should be evident that the predominant theme running through these views is an emphasis upon facilitating meaningful philosophic change for clients. In the following sections we detail how this emphasis is expressed in Ellis's positions on assessment and intervention procedures.

Assessment Procedures

With respect to assessment of client problems, Ellis espouses an approach that differs in several important respects from the approaches utilized by many mainstream practitioners of psychotherapy. First, he avoids extensive history-taking with clients. Secondly, he tends to avoid using standard diagnostic tests, particularly projective tests such as the Rorschach and the Thematic Apperception Test (TAT).

On the subject of extensive history-taking, Ellis has written the following:

> RET practitioners are not that interested in the details of what happened and in where and when it happened. Essentially, they are not too interested in past history. As a matter of fact, RET regards long-winded histories as irrelevant and side-tracking, for it sees this kind of narrative as having little or nothing to do with the client's present disturbances. Therefore, RET therapists encourage their clients to narrate their Activating Experiences in a relatively brief and nonobsessive manner. (1979e: 95)

Although he rejects the notion of extensive history-taking, Ellis (1968) gathers basic background information on clients by asking them to complete a Biographical Information Form (see pp. 74–7).

With respect to diagnostic tests, Ellis tends to favour objective personality questionnaires (the reader will recall that some of his earliest publications dealt with such measures) over projective techniques. He has noted that the latter 'often have dubious validity, incorporate questionable psychoanalytic and psychodynamic interpretations, and usually are not particularly relatable to effective treatment processes' (Ellis and Dryden, 1990: 151). Even objective tests, however, are not relied upon as the major means for understanding client problems and planning effective treatment.

Ellis holds the view that 'the best mode of diagnosis is therapy itself, since the ways in which the client reacts to the first few therapy sessions tells much more about him than any amount of objective or projective tests' (Saltzman and Ellis, 1986: 278). He has described the following advantages to this sort of therapy-based assessment (Ellis and Dryden, 1990).

1 It allows clients to immediately get to work on the problems that brought them to therapy, so that they can gain therapeutically while being assessed.

2 It assists therapists in determining which techniques to use with which clients. The therapist can observe how a particular client responds to a certain technique during an actual therapy session, and can decide on that basis whether to continue or discontinue use of that technique.

3 Assessment procedures employed in isolation from ongoing psychotherapy (as when a battery of tests is given to a client prior to starting therapy) may contribute to iatrogenic complications for some clients. If the assessment procedures are lengthy and take considerable time to complete, clients may

Date: _____   Name: _____
         mo.   day   yr.   (last)   (first)   (middle)

Biographical Information Form

Institute for Rational-Emotive Therapy
45 East 65th Street, New York, NY 10021

Instructions: To assist us in helping you, please fill out this form as frankly as you can. You will save much time and effort by giving us full information. You can be sure that, like everything you say at the Institute, the facts on this form will be held in the strictest confidence and no outsider will be permitted to see your case record without your written permission. PLEASE PRINT YOUR ANSWERS.

1. Date of birth: _____   Age: _____   Sex: M _____   F _____
                        mo.   day   yr.

2. Address: _____
                              street   city   state   zip code

3. Home phone: _____   Business phone: _____

4. Permanent address (if different from above): _____

   _____

5. Who referred you to the Institute? _____ (1) Self _____ (2) Family doctor _____ (3) Psychologist or psychiatrist

   _____ (4) Social agency _____ (5) Hospital or clinic _____ (6) School or teacher _____ (7) Friend

   _____ (8) Relative _____ (9) Other (explain) _____

   Has this party been here? _____ Yes _____ No

6. Present marital status: _____ (1) Never married _____ (2) (Married) (living together) now for first time

   _____ (3) (Married) (living together) now for second or more time _____ (4) Separated

   _____ (5) Divorced and not remarried _____ (6) Widowed and not remarried

   Number of years married to (or living with) present partner _____   Ages of sons _____   Ages of daughters _____

7. Years of formal education completed (Circle no. of years): 10 11 12 13 14 15 16 17 18 19 20 more than 20

8. How religious are you? (Circle number on scale that best approximates your degree of religiosity):

very			average			atheist	
1	2	3	4	5	6	7	8	9

9. Mother's age: _____   If deceased, how old were you when she died? _____

10. Father's age: _____   If deceased, how old were you when he died? _____

11. If your mother and father separated, how old were you at the time? _____

12. If your mother and father divorced, how old were you at the time? _____

13. Total number of times mother divorced _____   Number of times father divorced _____

14. Ages of living brothers _____   Ages of living sisters _____

15. I was child number _____ in a family of _____ children.

16. Were you adopted? _____ Yes _____ No

17. Have you ever had any individual psychotherapy or couples counseling? _____ Yes _____ No

    (Summarize approximate dates and length of treatment): _____

18. Have you ever attended group therapy? (List no. of months) _____

19. Have you ever been hospitalized for psychological problems? _____ Yes _____ No

20. Are you undergoing treatment anywhere else now? _____ Yes _____ No

21. Have you ever taken medication for emotional problems? _____ Yes _____ No

    If yes, specify the medications(s) and indicate whether you are currently taking it or when you *last* took it.

    _____

22. Type of psychotherapy you have mainly had (briefly describe method of treatment —e.g., dream analysis / free association, behavior therapy, cognitive therapy): _____

    _____

23. Briefly list (PRINT) your main complaints, symptoms, and problems: _____

    _____

    _____

    _____

24. Briefly list any additional past complaints, symptoms, and problems: _____

    _____

    _____

25. Under what conditions are your problems worse? _____

    _____

    _____

26. Under what conditions are they improved? _____

    _____

    _____

27. List the things you like to do most, the kinds of things and persons that give you pleasure: _____

    _____

    _____

28. List your main assets and good points: _____

    _____

    _____

29. List your main bad points: _____
_____
_____
_____

30. List your main **social** difficulties: _____
_____
_____

31. List your main **love and sex** difficulties: _____
_____
_____

32. List your main **school or work** difficulties: _____
_____
_____

33. List your main life goals: _____
_____
_____

34. List the things about yourself you would most like to change: _____
_____
_____

35. What would you ideally like your therapist to be able to give you? _____
_____
_____

35. List your chief physical ailments, diseases, complaints, or handicaps: _____
_____
_____

36. What occupation(s) have you mainly been trained for? _____

Present occupation: _____   _____ Full time   _____ Part time

37. Mate's occupation: _____   _____ Full time   _____ Part time

38. Mother's occupation: _____   Father's occupation: _____

39. Mother's religion: _____   Father's religion: _____

40. If your mother and father did not raise you when you were young, who did? _____

41. Briefly describe the type of person your mother (or stepmother or person who substituted for your mother) was when you were a child and her attitude toward you (past and present): _____

_____

_____

_____

42. Briefly describe the type of person your father (or stepfather or father substitute) was when you were a child and his attitude toward you (past and present): _____

_____

_____

_____

43. If there were any unusually disturbing features in your relationship to any of your brothers, briefly describe them:

_____

_____

44. If there were any unusually disturbing features in your relationship to any of your sisters, briefly describe them:

_____

_____

45. Close male relatives who have been seriously emotionally disturbed (specify): _____

Close male relatives that have been hospitalized for emotional problems or attempted suicide (specify): _____

Close female relatives who have been seriously emotionally disturbed (specify): _____

Close female relatives who that have been hospitalized for emotional problems or attempted suicide (specify): ____

46. Additional information that you think might be helpful: _____

_____

_____

_____

_____

_____

_____

_____

_____

_____

imagine 'horrors' about themselves that lead them astray and make it more difficult for them to benefit from therapy.

4 A number of conventional assessment devices – particularly projective devices like the Rorschach and the TAT – may falsely provide indications of symptoms and dynamics that clients really do not have. This can mislead therapists and result in unsuccessful or unnecessarily prolonged therapy.

5 Clients can sometimes be inclined to accept the results of complicated, arcane assessment procedures as representing the gospel truth, consequently believe that they now have a valid 'explanation' of what ails them, and incorrectly conclude that they have been helped by this 'expert' explanation. REBT assessment procedures focus on identifying what it is advisable for clients to do in order to change rather than emphasizing clever diagnostic explanations.

In terms of beginning therapy-oriented assessment, Ellis will typically ask clients during their initial session for a description of their major problem(s) (Ellis and Dryden, 1990). As clients describe their problems, Ellis works to quickly break down these problems according to their A, B and C components. If clients begin by describing A, then Ellis requests a description of C (their emotional and behavioural reactions to A). If, however, clients begin by outlining C, Ellis will ask for a brief description of A.

In line with his goal of conducting therapy as efficiently as is feasible, Ellis (1979e, 1991c) does not encourage clients to provide lengthy descriptions of their activating events or to compulsively talk about their feelings. With regard to lengthy descriptions of activating events, he has noted the following:

> Many clients, particularly those with prior psychoanalytic experience, love to describe the unfortunate Activating Events of their lives in long and gory detail. Sometimes this has a cathartic effect that helps them temporarily *feel* but not *get* better (Ellis, 1972b). Usually, it wastes time and encourages them to indulge in their miserable feeling. So for briefer and more effective RET, I try to help them to *summarize* their Activating Events and focus more on their irrational Beliefs and their emotional and behavioral Consequences. (Ellis, 1991c: 6)

With respect to avoiding compulsive talking about feelings, he has written that:

> Many clients, some of them trained to do so by previous therapy, long-windedly and compulsively talk about their feelings, their feelings, their feelings. Although they had better fully *acknowledge* these feelings and freely *express* them in therapy, endlessly obsessing about them and whining about them will do little good and sometimes much harm. I

usually say, after a few minutes of feeling talk, 'I fully understand that you feel very deeply about what's happening in your life, and I think that some of your strong feelings are quite appropriate and useful. But let's try to focus on your inappropriate and harmful feelings and what you're thinking and doing to create and maintain them. Let's get back to what you are irrationally thinking when you make yourself feel panicked, depressed, and self-hating.' (Ellis, 1991c: 6–7)

As the last sentence of the above excerpt suggests, Ellis is concerned with accurately and thoroughly assessing the nature of clients' irrational beliefs. Considering his accumulated experience (over four decades) in helping clients to uncover their patterns of faulty thinking, it is not surprising that he is quite adept at doing this. Usually, before a given client's initial session is even half over, Ellis will advance a number of hypotheses concerning the irrational beliefs that may underpin the individual's emotional and behavioural problems. These hypotheses are generally expressed aloud to the client, for at least two reasons: (1) they serve as a vehicle for teaching clients to be aware of the relationship between their thoughts and their feelings, and (2) they provide an opportunity for Ellis to gauge the accuracy of his clinical hunches through observation of the client's reactions to his statements. The latter reason has particular relevance for the process of rational-emotive assessment, as Ellis will not hesitate to question a given hypothesis when confronted with sufficient evidence of its invalidity. When a hunch proves to be inaccurate, he continues the process of listening, observing and advancing hypotheses until he believes he is probably on target (Yankura and Dryden, 1990).

Ellis often manages to identify clients' operative irrational beliefs quite quickly. After determining a given client's emotional and behavioural C's, he draws inferences concerning the types of irrational beliefs that could be implicated in these C's (Yankura and Dryden, 1990). He will, for example, speculate that an angry client is holding rigid demands about the manner in which other people *should* behave, while an anxious client may be subscribing to the idea that certain possible future events would be *awful* and therefore *must not* occur. Ellis uses his knowledge of a particular client's inappropriate C's to track down operative irrational beliefs. It is important to note that Ellis's approach to assessment does not merely occupy some circumscribed segment of therapy (such as the initial session); rather, he considers assessment to be an ongoing part of the therapeutic process. Thus, over the course of treatment, he may decide that it is appropriate to shift the focus of therapy to more pernicious irrationalities that may not have been evident during a client's early sessions (Ellis and Dryden, 1990).

Ellis also uses the therapy-oriented approach to assessment as a means for formulating hypotheses as to the treatment methods likely to work best with particular clients. In particular, Ellis will monitor client responses to his early attempts at intervention during sessions in order to determine (a) how seriously disturbed the clients are, (b) how difficult clients may be to work with and how they will take to the main REBT procedures and (c) what type of therapist involvement (for example, a very forceful and confrontational therapist stance versus a somewhat more relaxed, supportive one) will be most beneficial to clients (Ellis and Dryden, 1990; Yankura and Dryden, 1990). He may, for instance, decide to employ a forceful and active disputing style with some seriously disturbed clients who have well-entrenched irrational beliefs (Ellis, 1985c). With certain intellectually limited clients, he may choose to mainly abandon attempts at philosophical disputing in favour of teaching these individuals to make effective use of rational self-statements. With seriously depressed, suicidal individuals, he may decide to utilize more warmth and support (until some progress has been made in overcoming the depression) than he would generally tend to do with less disturbed clients (Dryden and Ellis, 1985).

Having now outlined Ellis's approach to assessment within REBT, we turn to consideration of his major contributions concerning intervention procedures.

Intervention Procedures

As noted previously, Ellis encourages his clients, whenever feasible, to make lasting, profound philosophical changes that will help them to both minimize their current upsets and make them less vulnerable to future disturbance. Generally, he begins a course of treatment with the hypothesis that a given client will be able to achieve such change (Ellis and Dryden, 1990). He attempts, therefore, to employ the strategies and techniques of preferential REBT. This, of course, involves swiftly moving to help the client to identify and dispute irrational beliefs. If, however, the client's early responses to treatment suggest that profound philosophical change is not a feasible goal, Ellis will switch tack and employ alternative methods for helping to relieve the client from emotional distress. Such a change in strategy is in line with his therapy-oriented approach to assessment.

Ellis (1979e) advocates a multi-modal approach to psychotherapy, as he believes that clients will experience greater success in effecting cognitive change if their dysfunctional ideas and attitudes are attacked on a variety of dimensions and in a number of different ways. In his own clinical work, he utilizes techniques targeted at the cognitive, behavioural and emotive dimensions of clients' psychological functioning. Ellis (1979e: 66) recommends that therapists employ flexibility and creativity in choosing which therapeutic techniques to use, with the proviso that 'these methods are used in [an] . . . RET philosophical framework and are not employed in a hit-or-miss manner because the therapist has some vague idea that they might work with certain clients'.

In the following sections, we review some of the main cognitive, behavioural and emotive methods that Ellis utilizes in his work with clients. Throughout these presentations, we will place an emphasis upon methods that Ellis himself has created (or particularly refined) for use in his clinical practice. These methods can thus be regarded as representing unique contributions to the fields of psychotherapy and counselling. We acknowledge that dividing interventions into cognitive, behavioural and emotive categories is a somewhat artificial contrivance, as there can be considerable overlap with respect to the modalities targeted by a particular technique. Ultimately, most of the techniques utilized and espoused by Ellis are intended to have a beneficial impact on the cognitive, philosophical dimension of clients' functioning. Nevertheless, the categorical scheme we employ will help to highlight the multi-modal quality of the intervention procedures which Ellis uses in his practice of REBT.

Cognitive Methods
Usually, right at the very start of treatment, Ellis places a strong emphasis on teaching clients how to identify and dispute their irrational beliefs (Yankura and Dryden, 1990). He has written that:

> The most elegant and probably the most common cognitive method of RET consists of the therapist's actively-directively Disputing the client's irrational Beliefs. If there is any fundamental rational-emotive method, this is probably it. So much so, in fact, that some commentators on RET wrongly assume that the Disputing or Debating process (sometimes called 'anti-awfulizing' or 'anti*mus*turbation') *is* RET (Mahoney, 1979; Meichenbaum, 1979). It definitely is not! But if RET were totally devoid of this kind of Disputing, it would be almost unrecognizable. (Ellis, 1979e: 67)

By actively disputing clients' irrational beliefs within sessions, Ellis models disputing procedures. He teaches clients to analyse their emotional and behavioural problems within the ABC framework, and strongly encourages them to practise disputing procedures on an independent basis, both within and outside of therapy sessions. As described in Chapter 2, he will sometimes teach clients to

employ a particular format for disputing, such as the one represented in DIBs (disputing irrational beliefs) (Ellis, 1979e). More
generally, he will show clients how to make use of a variety of
disputing questions when they experience an upset and have
identified their operative irrational beliefs (Yankura and Dryden,
1990).

Review of audiotapes of Ellis's therapy sessions suggests that he
makes use of at least three main types of disputing arguments with
his clients (DiGiuseppe, 1991):

1 *Logical disputing*: With this type of disputing argument,
   clients are helped to understand the illogical nature of their
   irrational beliefs. Often, logical disputing involves showing
   clients that just because they believe certain conditions would
   be preferable or desirable, these conditions do not *have to* exist.
   Thus, logical disputing arguments tend to underscore the fact
   that escalating one's preference (or rational belief) to the level
   of an absolutistic demand (or irrational belief) represents an
   illogical *non sequitur*. The following is an example of a logical
   disputing question that Ellis might use with a given client:
   'Granted, it would be better if the boss were to treat you and
   the other employees more fairly – but does it follow that she
   absolutely *has to* do the preferable thing?'

2 *Empirical disputing*: The goal of this type of disputing
   argument is to demonstrate to clients that their absolutistic
   demands (with their associated derivatives of awfulizing, I-
   can't-stand-it-itis, and negative person-rating) are almost always
   inconsistent with reality. As an example of an empirical
   disputing question, Ellis would ask a client, 'Where is the
   evidence that you *must* succeed?' In essence, the client is being
   asked to provide evidence in support of her irrational belief.
   Using empirical disputing, the client could be shown that there
   is no sound evidence to support her *must* – after all, if it were
   true that she *must* succeed, she would always have to succeed
   under any and all conditions, regardless of what she happened
   to believe.

3 *Pragmatic disputing*: This type of disputing argument focuses
   on showing clients the practical (in this context, emotional and
   behavioural) consequences of holding irrational beliefs. Here,
   the goal is to show clients that as long as they subscribe to their
   absolutistic demands (with their associated derivatives), they
   are likely to remain disturbed. In conducting pragmatic
   disputing, Ellis would pose the following sort of question to a
   client: 'If you continue to believe that you *have to* do well on

your exams, what's it going to get you?' (Pause for client's
response.) 'That's right – anxious!'

Ellis also makes use of the following cognitive methods for
assisting clients in the process of challenging and replacing their
irrational beliefs.

Structured Disputing. In addition to the DIBs format, Ellis has
also designed a number of worksheets that clients can utilize for
structured disputing of their irrational beliefs. In his psychotherapy
practice at the Institute for Rational-Emotive Therapy in New
York City, he routinely makes available to his clients an RET Self-
Help Form (see pp. 84–5) that he encourages them to complete
between sessions as a cognitive homework assignment (Sichel and
Ellis, 1984). This form, which is organized according to the ABC
framework, first requires clients to write a brief description of
their relevant activating events and emotional/behavioural consequences with respect to a given episode of emotional upset or self-
defeating behaviour. Clients next identify their operative irrational
beliefs (by choosing those that apply from a list of common
irrational beliefs that is provided), and then construct disputing
questions for challenging each one. They write their responses to
these disputing questions in a column labelled 'E' for 'Effective
Rational Beliefs', and finally note down the (ideally less self-
defeating) feelings and behaviours they experienced after arriving
at their effective rational beliefs. It is noted that this worksheet
ends with a statement intended to encourage clients to work
vigorously and repeatedly at practising a new rational philosophy:
'I will work hard to repeat my effective rational beliefs forcefully
to myself on many occasions so that I can make myself less
disturbed now and act less self-defeatingly in the future.' This
statement is related to the third main insight of REBT (Ellis,
1977d) as described in Chapter 2.

Rational Self-statements. With intellectually limited clients, or as a
temporary supplement with clients who are in the process of
acquiring disputation skills, Ellis (1979e; Ellis and Dryden, 1990)
will sometimes encourage practice of rational self-statements.
Rational self-statements will often reflect a person's desires and
preferences with respect to some personally meaningful issue, and
are used to directly counter the rigid shoulds and musts that the
individual typically brings to bear upon this issue. Ellis (1979e: 82)
has described his use of rational self-statements in his case
description of Myra, a female client who presented with the

RET SELF-HELP FORM

Institute for Rational-Emotive Therapy
45 East 65th Street, New York, NY 10021
(212) 535-0822

(A) ACTIVATING EVENTS, thoughts, or feelings that happened just before I felt emotionally disturbed or acted self-defeatingly:

_____

(C) CONSEQUENCE OR CONDITION—disturbed feeling or self-defeating behavior—that I produced and would like to change:

_____

(B) BELIEFS—Irrational BELIEFS (iBs) leading to my CONSEQUENCE (emotional disturbance or self-defeating behavior). Circle all that apply to these ACTIVATING EVENTS (A).	(D) DISPUTES for each circled Irrational BELIEF (iB). Examples: *"Why MUST I do very well?" "Where is it written* that I am a BAD PERSON?" *"Where is the evidence* that I MUST be approved or accepted?"	(E) EFFECTIVE RATIONAL BELIEFS (RBs) to replace my Irrational BELIEFS (iBs). Examples: "I'd PREFER to do very well *but I don't* HAVE TO." "I am a PERSON WHO acted badly, *not* a BAD PERSON." *"There is no evidence* that I HAVE TO be approved, though I would LIKE to be."
1. I MUST do well or very well!		
2. I am a BAD OR WORTHLESS PERSON when I act weakly or stupidly.		
3. I MUST be approved or accepted by people I find important!		
4. I NEED to be loved by someone who matters to me a lot!		
5. I am a BAD, UNLOVABLE PERSON if I get rejected.		
6. People MUST treat me fairly and give me what I NEED!		

(OVER)

7. People MUST live up to my expectations or it is TERRIBLE!		
8. People who act immorally are undeserving, ROTTEN PEOPLE!		
9. I CAN'T STAND really bad things or very difficult people!		
10. My life MUST have few major hassles or troubles.		
11. It's AWFUL or HORRIBLE when major things don't go my way!		
12. I CAN'T STAND IT when life is really unfair!		
13. I NEED a good deal of immediate gratification and HAVE to feel miserable when I don't get it!		
Additional Irrational Beliefs:		

(F) FEELINGS and BEHAVIORS I experience after arriving at my EFFECTIVE RATIONAL BELIEFS: _____

I WILL WORK HARD TO REPEAT MY EFFECTIVE RATIONAL BELIEFS FORCEFULLY TO MYSELF ON MANY OCCASIONS SO THAT I CAN MAKE MYSELF LESS DISTURBED NOW AND ACT LESS SELF-DEFEATINGLY IN THE FUTURE.

Joyce Sichel, Ph.D. and Albert Ellis, Ph.D.
Copyright © 1984 by the Institute for Rational-Emotive Therapy.

100 forms $10.00
1000 forms $80.00

primary symptom of being inorgasmic and the secondary symptom of global negative self-rating (with reference to her 'poor' sexual functioning):

> after working on discovering a good many of her *shoulds* and *musts* . . . Myra was encouraged to replace them with nonabsolutistic preferences and wishes. For several weeks she carried around 3 x 5 cards with her on which she had written such statements as 'I don't *have to* achieve orgasm but still definitely would *like* to do so,' 'I don't *need* what I want,' and 'I'd better give up all my *shoulds*.' She would look at these cards several times each day and think about their messages until they began to sink into her head.

Ellis (1979e; Ellis and Dryden, 1990) favours disputing over the use of rational self-statements because it's probably more likely to contribute to deep-seated philosophical change, but recognizes that not all clients will be able to attain this level of change. Practice of rational self-statements can therefore represent a means for more limited clients to access and utilize a rational philosophy.

Using REBT with Others.   Ellis (1979e, 1984c) often suggests to clients that they engage in *rational proselytizing*, wherein they use REBT to help friends and relatives with *their* problems. This is based upon his recognition that humans can facilitate their own learning by *doing* and by teaching others. With respect to recommending this particular cognitive method to clients, Ellis has written:

> Practice using RET with some of your friends, relatives, or associates who are willing to let you try to help them with it. The more often you use it with others, and are able to see what their iBs are and to try to talk them out of these self-defeating ideas, the more you will be able to understand the main principles of RET and to use them with yourself. When you see other people act irrationally and in a disturbed manner, try to figure out – with or without talking to them about it – what their main irrational beliefs probably are and how these could be actively and vigorously disputed. (1984c: 3)

It is noted that Ellis advises clients to use REBT with other individuals who are *amenable* to being 'therapized', as he is aware that unsolicited attempts to apply therapy to one's associates are not always welcome. Incidentally, Ellis regards the technique of using REBT with others to be one of the most powerful therapeutic elements of the therapy groups he leads, as clients in these groups often become better at challenging their own irrational beliefs when they work at helping to challenge the irrational beliefs of other group members.

Biblio- and Audiotherapy. Quite frequently, Ellis suggests to his clients that they obtain and use some of the REBT psycho-educational materials that are available for the general public. In an article reviewing Ellis's responses to a broad survey of rational emotive behaviour therapists (Warren, McLellarn and Ellis, 1987), Ellis indicated that he employs bibliotherapy with 100 per cent of his clients. By his own report, the self-help books he most frequently recommends are: (a) *How to Stubbornly Refuse to Make Yourself Miserable about Anything – Yes, Anything* (Ellis, 1988b), suggested to 95 per cent of clients; (b) *A New Guide to Rational Living* (Ellis and Harper, 1975), suggested to 90 per cent of clients; (c) *A Guide to Personal Happiness* (Ellis and Becker, 1982), suggested to 95 per cent of clients and (d) *Overcoming Procrastination* (Ellis and Knaus, 1977), suggested to 40 per cent of clients. By reviewing and studying REBT psychoeducational materials, clients can give themselves a foundation in rational-emotive principles and techniques, help themselves to internalize a rational philosophy and potentially hasten their progress in therapy. REBT-oriented audiotapes often present a helpful alternative to bibliotherapy for clients who have relatively poor reading skills.

Reviewing Audiotapes of Sessions. Ellis routinely encourages his clients to tape-record their therapy sessions with him (Ellis and Dryden, 1990). They can then independently review these audiotapes at a later time. Such reviews can be quite valuable from a therapeutic perspective, as it allows opportunities for clients to re-hear Ellis's disputing arguments. Material that may not have had much of an impact at the time of a particular session can sometimes make a considerable impression on clients when it is heard (and more closely attended to) subsequent to the session.

Behavioural Methods
Ellis incorporates a good number of active, behavioural methods within his clinical practice. His emphasis on utilizing such methods dates back to his early experiences as a marital and sex therapist, when he found it particularly helpful 'to supplement the therapy sessions with specific instructions to the clients with regard to what they were supposed to do with themselves and others in between sessions' (Ellis, 1979e: 91). He favours behavioural methods within his REBT practice because he recognizes that cognitive change is very often facilitated by behavioural change (Ellis and Dryden, 1990). As will be seen, a good number of the behavioural methods employed by Ellis involve encouraging clients to expose themselves

(or risk exposing themselves) to problematic A's. Ellis particularly encourages his clients to undertake such exposure on an implosive basis, as opposed to pursuing the sort of graduated exposure endorsed by a number of behaviour therapists. As per the earlier discussion on implosive methods, this is because Ellis (1979b, 1980a, 1990a) sees these methods as potentially more efficient and effective for clients. Also, utilization of implosive methods is viewed by Ellis as being less likely to inadvertently reinforce the irrational beliefs underpinning clients' discomfort disturbance.

Shame-attacking Exercises.   In this behavioural method, clients are encouraged to purposely engage in silly and outlandish (but non-harmful to self and others) behaviours in a public venue (Ellis, 1969; Ellis and Becker, 1982). The purpose of this exercise is for clients to provide themselves with an opportunity to (a) work at not taking the disapproval of other individuals *over*seriously, and (b) to work at accepting themselves even when they act in a 'shameful' fashion. During the course of conducting a shame-attacking exercise, clients also often learn that other people frequently do not verbally attack others who are perceived to be acting in some foolish way. Some of the shame-attacking exercises that Ellis routinely suggests to his clients (when seen as appropriate to the individual's treatment) include the following:

1 Asking for a gross of condoms at a pharmacy counter, and then requesting a discount because one uses so many.
2 Loudly announcing the stops on the subway (without fleeing the car one happens to be in).
3 Stopping a stranger on the street and saying, 'Excuse me, I've just gotten out of the loony bin. Can you tell me what year it is?'

Clients who agree to undertake shame-attacking exercises are, of course, cautioned not to engage in behaviours that may unduly alarm others, cause the clients to lose their jobs, or cause them to be arrested by the police.

Risk-taking Exercises. In risk-taking exercises, clients push themselves to take calculated risks in areas where they wish to make changes (Ellis and Dryden, 1990). As an example of a risk-taking exercise, Ellis cites his experience of forcing himself to approach and speak with a hundred individual women in the Bronx Botanical Gardens (see Chapter 1). Often, when clients push themselves to undertake such an exercise, they learn in a very powerful way that the outcomes they fear are not at all 'awful' (even when these feared outcomes actually *do* occur, since sometimes they do not) and that they are quite well able to handle them. In addition to helping clients to de-awfulize feared outcomes, it is noted that risk-taking exercises can occasionally have positive side-effects for clients. As an example, a young woman with evaluative anxiety who forces herself to repeatedly engage in public speaking will not only overcome her awfulizing about the possibility that her audience won't approve of her; she will also probably become a better public speaker simply through practice (Yankura and Dryden, 1990).

'Stay in There' Activities. First described as 'stay in there' activities by Grieger and Boyd (1980), these exercises require clients to stay in situations typically experienced as emotionally uncomfortable while disputing their beliefs that they are absolutely unable to tolerate this discomfort. Clients who undertake these exercises fully 'court discomfort' in order to prove to themselves that they *can* stand it. As an example, a young woman who loathes seeing her mother-in-law because she feels that she subjects her to constant criticism might take on the homework assignment of *purposely* arranging a day-long visit with her. During the visit, she would dispute her irrational beliefs that 'I *can't stand* my mother-in-law's constant criticisms; she absolutely *should not* put me down as much as she does.'

Anti-procrastination Exercises. Ellis (Ellis and Knaus, 1977) has pointed out that procrastination can often be a product of discomfort anxiety. Individuals convince themselves that the discomfort involved in accomplishing certain tasks is too much to bear, and that they *shouldn't* have to experience such discomfort. They then tend to engage in avoidance of the task in question (that is, they procrastinate). Anti-procrastination exercises require clients to expose themselves to 'unbearable' tasks, while pushing themselves to tolerate the discomfort involved in the task. By doing so, they can provide themselves with concrete evidence that they can indeed deal with discomfort and accomplish an avoided activity. As an example of an anti-procrastination exercise, a student who had been avoiding work on her doctoral dissertation might be encouraged to push herself to spend a pre-determined amount of time each day working on it. By implementing such a regimen, she could provide herself with an opportunity to dispute the irrational beliefs behind her discomfort anxiety and show herself that she can tolerate uncomfortable feelings.

Use of Rewards and Penalties.   In order to encourage his clients to undertake challenging homework assignments, Ellis will suggest to them that they identify and utilize personally meaningful rewards and penalties (Ellis, 1979e: Ellis and Dryden, 1990; Yankura and Dryden, 1990). Clients reward themselves with some pleasurable thing or activity only *after* they have accomplished a particular homework activity; if they fail to do their homework, they give themselves some sort of obnoxious, unpleasant penalty. Thus, a client who has been procrastinating on some important task might agree to allow himself to engage in pleasure reading (a personally meaningful reward) only after he has worked on the task for some pre-specified period of time. If he fails to work on the task as specified by the end of a given day, he would penalize himself by purposely undertaking some activity that he strongly dislikes (such as thoroughly cleaning the bathroom at 11.00 PM, before allowing himself to go to bed). Ellis (1979e, 1985c) has noted that for clients who agree to apply them, the utilization of rewards and penalties can represent a very useful means for helping clients to do difficult homework assignments. He has found that stiff penalties can be particularly useful with chronically resistant clients (Ellis, 1985c).

As noted earlier, Ellis's use of behavioural techniques is aimed at facilitating meaningful philosophic change for clients. With clients who have difficulty approaching the goal of philosophic change, however, behavioural techniques can still be useful insofar as they provide important opportunities for skills practice.

Emotive Methods

From time to time, Ellis has been subjected to criticisms that he neglects the emotive aspects of psychotherapy. Such criticisms are quite inaccurate, as Ellis employs numerous emotive techniques in his work with clients. Some of the ones he has detailed in his writings include the following.

Unconditional Acceptance of Clients.   The importance of offering clients unconditional acceptance has been described in previous sections. Ellis (1979e) routinely offers his clients such acceptance during the course of therapy, as he believes it helps them to accept *themselves* with their human fallibilities and failings. He will not hesitate, however, to bring obnoxious behaviour to clients' attention when doing so may help them to function better in their relationships with others. When he does so, he is careful to ensure that clients (a) do not mistakenly perceive that he is damning them in their totality, and (b) do not damn themselves for engaging in behaviours regarded by others as quite obnoxious.

Therapist Self-disclosure. When employed properly, therapist self-disclosure can have a strong emotional impact on clients. Ellis will utilize this technique to model a rational philosophy to his clients (Ellis and Dryden, 1990). He will make reference to an emotional problem he once experienced (such as the shyness or the public speaking anxiety he had earlier in life), and describe how he utilized rational-emotive methods and philosophy to overcome this problem. In being open in this manner, he indirectly conveys to clients that they don't have to rate themselves negatively for their own emotional problems. He also provides an actual example of how REBT can be effectively utilized to overcome such difficulties. This can inspire hope in clients, and prompt them to think about how they might apply REBT to resolve their own problems.

Humorous Techniques. As another emotive means to challenge the irrational beliefs to which clients subscribe, Ellis will employ a variety of techniques that embody a humorous quality. He has found that such methods can be quite useful in helping clients to see the illogical and frequently contradictory nature of their irrational beliefs in a light-hearted way. Thus, he will employ exaggerated terminology, humorously amplify the absurdity of clients' irrational beliefs, and relate humorous stories and slogans which serve to underscore the fatuous nature of certain types of irrational thinking (Yankura and Dryden, 1990). Ellis (1977a, 1987d) has also composed a number of rational humorous songs which clients can use to challenge their irrational beliefs in a particularly unique and evocative way. The lyrics of these songs lampoon a particular type of irrational thinking, and they are set to a variety of popular tunes. The following rational humorous song (set to the tune of 'Funiculi, Funicula' by Luigi Denza) can be especially meaningful for clients who turn their *preference* to think rationally into an absolute demand:

Perfect Rationality

Some think the world must have a right direction
And so do I! And so do I!
Some think that, with the slightest imperfection
They can't get by – and so do I!
For I, I have to prove I'm superhuman,
And better far than people are!
To show I have miraculous acumen –
And always rate among the Great!
Perfect, perfect rationality
Is, of course, the only thing for me!

How can I ever think of being
If I must live fallibly?
Rationality must be a perfect thing for me!
(Lyrics by Albert Ellis, copyrighted 1977
by the Institute for Rational-Emotive Therapy)

Use of Passionate Rational Self-statements. Clients can challenge their irrational beliefs in an especially emotive, evocative fashion by employing passionate rational self-statements (Ellis, 1979e). Passionate rational self-statements consist of vigorous, dramatic self-verbalizations such as 'I'd like to be accepted by the people I meet at the party, but if I'm not, it's just *too damn bad*! Fuck it! I don't NEED the approval of others in order to accept myself!' Ellis often advocates that his clients use these sorts of statements for two major reasons: (a) irrational beliefs are often deeply rooted and can tend to remain so unless they are powerfully challenged (Ellis, 1985c), and (b) what we refer to as 'emotions' are at least partly derived from quite dramatic and vehement self-verbalizations (Ellis, 1979e). The emotions we experience are thus influenced by the manner in which we talk to ourselves.

Therapist's Judicious Use of Profanity. Ellis often models the use of passionate rational self-statements to clients during his therapy sessions, in part by selectively employing profanity as he works to dispute irrational beliefs. He will utilize 'four-letter words' to add emphasis to points that he wishes to make; also, he views profane language as a vehicle for breaking down the barriers to intimacy that can exist between the therapist and certain types of clients (Ellis, 1977a, 1985c). Here, it is noted that individuals may generally restrict their use of profanity to their relationships with their closest associates. Ellis, however, does not employ profanity indiscriminately during therapy; he may, for instance, abandon its use when he notes that a given client has a negative response to it (Yankura and Dryden, 1990).

Rational-emotive Imagery. When using this technique, Ellis (1979e; Maultsby and Ellis, 1974) asks clients to close their eyes and imagine, as vividly as they can, an activating event which for them is usually associated with an unhealthy negative emotion. After calling up an image of this situation or event, clients are then encouraged to allow themselves to experience the typical upsetting feeling with which they respond to this activating event. Once they signal to Ellis that they have attained this negative feeling, he gives them a simple directive to change their unhealthy negative emotion into a healthy negative emotion without modifying the image in any way (for example, 'Now, change your feeling of anger to a feeling of annoyance at this person's *act* but not damnation of *them* for acting that way'). When they indicate that they have done so, Ellis queries them as to how they accomplished this shift in their feelings. By doing so, he hopes to prompt clients into noting that the change in their feelings was attributable to a change in their manner of thinking about the problematic activating event. Ideally, this change in thinking will represent a shift from irrational beliefs to rational beliefs. Ellis routinely utilizes rational-emotive imagery during public demonstrations of rational emotive behaviour therapy with volunteer 'clients' (as at his regular Friday evening workshop, 'Problems of Daily Living', given at the Institute for Rational-Emotive Therapy in New York City). He recommends to clients that they practise this technique daily for about a month in order to achieve beneficial results. The goal of such practice is to 'automatically' have healthy instead of unhealthy negative feelings when they imagine (or actually experience) very bad activating events.

Dealing with Resistance in Psychotherapy

Resistance is a commonly encountered (and often quite perplexing) phenomenon within counselling and psychotherapy. It is probably safe to say that all veteran mental health practitioners have at one time or another worked with clients who appear to sabotage themselves by resisting the therapist's ministrations and by creating seemingly ingenious obstacles to 'getting better'. Over the course of his long career as a psychotherapist, Ellis has developed a perspective on the phenomenon of resistance that can be considered rather unique within the mental health field. It is summarized in the following passage:

> Rational-emotive therapy (RET), together with cognitive-behavioral therapy (CBT), assumes that when clients self-defeatingly and irrationally resist following therapeutic procedures and homework assignments, they largely do so because of their explicit and implicit cognitions or beliefs. RET, which tends to be more philosophical and persuasive than some other forms of CBT . . . assumes that resisting clients have an underlying set of powerful and persistent irrational beliefs (iB's) as well as an innate biosocial tendency to create new irrationalities, that frequently block them from carrying out the therapeutic goals and contracts that they overtly agree to work at achieving. Although RET does not agree with psychoanalytic and psychodynamic theory, which holds that client resistance is based on deeply unconscious, repressed thoughts and feelings, it does hypothesize

that many – perhaps most – of the iB's that underlie client resistance are (1) at least partially implicit, unconscious, or automatic; (2) tenaciously held; (3) held concomitantly with strong feelings and fixed habit patterns of behavior; (4) to some extent held by virtually all clients; (5) difficult to change; and (6) likely to recur once they have been temporarily surrendered ... RET practitioners are largely concerned with helping resisters (and other clients) make a profound philosophic change so that they adopt a cooperative, confident, determined attitude toward self-change, rather than the self-blocking views that they hold. (Ellis, 1990b: 267–8)

The above quote focuses on resistance that stems from factors internal to the client. As will be seen, however, Ellis does not exclusively restrict his focus to client factors. He is also alert to resistance that can be attributed to therapist factors as well as to factors that relate to aspects of the relationship between client and therapist.

Despite a longstanding interest in the problem of resistance, Ellis had not written extensively on this topic until Windy Dryden asked him to do an article on it in 1983 for the *British Journal of Cognitive Psychotherapy*. Ellis subsequently produced not just one article on resistance, but four. He later expanded on these articles and published them in book form as *Overcoming Resistance: Rational-Emotive Therapy with Difficult Clients* (Ellis, 1985c). In his writings, Ellis has identified the following types of resistance as being fairly common within psychotherapy and counselling.

'Healthy' Resistance.   Ellis (1985c, 1990b) notes that therapists may sometimes try to impose inaccurate conceptualizations of symptoms or false interpretations upon clients. When clients refuse to accept their therapists' erroneous views on these issues, he describes them as engaging in 'healthy' resistance. While Ellis (1982) believes that psychoanalytically trained therapists may often attempt to foist false interpretations upon their clients, he recognizes that rational emotive behavioural and cognitive-behavioural therapists can also be guilty of committing similar sorts of errors (as when an REBT counsellor incorrectly tries to convince a particular client that she subscribes to certain types of irrational beliefs). Ellis (1990b) encourages therapists and counsellors to monitor themselves and to seek regular supervision so that they can avoid arousing this category of resistance in their clients.

Resistance Due to Client/Therapist Mismatching.   Ellis (1985c, 1990b) notes that clients may sometimes pick or be assigned to a therapist who presents characteristics that they dislike. When this is the case, it becomes more difficult to establish and maintain a working therapeutic alliance, and resistance can occur. Ellis (1985c, 1990b) observes that this situation can be resolved in three main ways: (a) therapists try to compensate for the 'flaws' their clients perceive in them (for example, by working extra hard or by offering more warmth than they normally would), (b) clients overcome their prejudices against their therapists as therapy proceeds, or (c) clients and/or therapists choose to terminate the therapeutic relationship (perhaps with referral to a more 'appropriate' practitioner).

Resistance Stemming from Clients' Transference Disturbances. Ellis (1985c, 1990b) believes that disturbed transference relationships will *sometimes* but not *necessarily* occur within psychotherapy. When they do occur, resistance can result. 'Thus,' Ellis (1990b: 270) writes, 'if a young woman has a middle-aged male analyst, she [may] strongly tend to fall in love with him (as she presumably once loved her father), [may then] be jealous of his wife and hate him when he refuses to go to bed with her, [and may] try to control him as she tried to control her father, and so forth.' Ellis (1985c, 1990b) views disturbed transference relationships as stemming from particular irrational beliefs that clients may hold. He advises therapists to be alert for such beliefs, so that they can help clients to recognize and surmount them.

Resistance Due to Therapists' Relationship Problems. Ellis (1985c, 1990b) notes that therapists, like clients, can also sometimes have relationship difficulties. When this is so, it is important for therapists to take note of their own limitations and to compensate accordingly. In particular, therapists can look for and dispute their own counter-transference-producing irrational beliefs, so that they overcome any tendency they may have to be inappropriately prejudiced against certain clients.

Resistance Related to Therapists' Moralistic Attitudes. According to Ellis (1985c, 1990b), it can be fairly common for therapists and counsellors to hold irrational beliefs that lead them to condemn themselves and/or others for bad or foolish acts. When they apply such beliefs to their clients, they may openly or covertly damn them for engaging in obnoxious behaviour (for example, arriving late for sessions; refusing to pay bills). As a result, they may inadvertently prompt these clients to increase their own self-damning tendencies so that they become more (instead of less) disturbed. Clients exposed to global condemnation by their therapists may naturally resist the therapeutic process. Since rational emotive behaviour therapists strive to offer unconditional acceptance to their clients, they work to extirpate the irrational beliefs that may block them from doing so.

Resistance Linked to Client/Therapist Love–Hate Problems.   Ellis (1985c, 1990b) notes that the feelings clients and therapists develop towards each other may have nothing to do with transference/counter-transference issues. Thus, a female client may realistically fall in love with her therapist because he truly possesses traits that (in her view) may characterize a good potential partner. Similarly, therapists may in some cases fall in love with their clients. In certain scenarios, client and/or therapist may act to prolong the therapy in order to maintain contact with the individual with whom they are in love. Ellis observes that non-transference relationship feelings that encourage resistance can be difficult to resolve, since they are mainly reality-based. They can, however, be partly related to particular irrational beliefs that can be identified and disputed. When these beliefs are effectively countered, the motivation for the resistance may be largely removed.

Resistance Related to Fear of Disclosure.   Ellis (1985c, 1990b) states that this is one of the most common forms of resistance. Clients frequently resist being open in therapy because they find it emotionally uncomfortable to speak about thoughts, feelings, and actions that they consider 'shameful'. Their feelings of shame, of course, stem from irrational beliefs concerning internal standards that *must* be met in order to regard oneself as a 'good' person. Also, clients are sometimes afraid to confess misdeeds in therapy because they believe that they *must* maintain the approval and support of their therapists. Ellis (1985c, 1990b) advocates quickly showing clients how to recognize and dispute the beliefs that create obstacles to self-disclosure, so that they are better able to assume the risks of being open and honest in therapy.

Resistance Created by Fear of Discomfort.   Ellis (1985c, 1990b) identifies this category as representing the most common and strongest type of resistance encountered in psychotherapy. It stems from low frustration tolerance, or discomfort disturbance as Ellis (1979b, 1980a) has termed it. Clients who have discomfort disturbance about their therapy will often avoid the hard work involved in making therapeutic gains. Irrational demands for comfort, certainty and immediate gratification within therapy can underpin this form of resistance; clients can be helped to overcome it when they are taught how to dispute these absolutistic demands.

Secondary Gain Resistance. Experienced therapists of various theoretical orientations note that some clients appear to resist changing because they derive certain pay-offs (or manage to avoid particular 'penalties') by remaining disturbed. Thus, a depressive individual may resist improving because it would mean losing the sympathy and support of family members and friends. A non-assertive woman may resist becoming more assertive because the males in her interpersonal environment would tend to respond negatively to an assertive female. When working with individuals who resist therapy because of secondary gains, Ellis (1985c, 1990b) would attempt to help them uncover and challenge their irrational beliefs about improving in therapy and losing the supposed pay-offs that such change (in their perception) may entail.

Resistance Stemming from Feelings of Hopelessness. Ellis (1962, 1979b, 1980a) notes that clients' thoughts and feelings about the hopelessness of ever overcoming their disturbance represents a particular form of secondary disturbance. An anxious client, for example, may make some initial progress in therapy and then experience some backsliding. This client may then irrationally conclude, 'My backsliding proves that I'm an *utterly hopeless case*; I'll *never* be able to conquer my problems!' This conclusion, of course, would tend to discourage the client from making continued and persistent efforts at self-help within therapy. As discussed in Chapter 2, Ellis advises rational emotive behaviour therapists to be particularly alert for clients' secondary symptoms, so that these can be dealt with swiftly and effectively.

Resistance Motivated by Self-punishment. Ellis (1990b) notes that while he has rarely encountered this type of resistance in his work with neurotic clients, he occasionally comes across it when working with psychotic and severely borderline individuals. He observes that it tends to stem from irrational beliefs such as the following: 'Because I have acted poorly and/or have engaged in evil acts, which I absolutely *should not* have done, I am a thoroughly *worthless individual* who deserves to suffer! I therefore *deserve* to be continually disturbed and will make no real effort to use therapy to help myself.' Ellis advocates that therapists actively and directively help clients to recognize and surrender these resistance-creating beliefs.

Resistance Motivated by Fear of Change or Fear of Success. Ellis (1985c, 1990b) has observed that a good number of clients resist changing because they have self-created 'needs' for safety and certainty. Thus, although they find their symptoms to be uncomfortable, they are at least accustomed to them and may fear that if they lose them they may experience even *greater* discomfort. Ellis (1990b) also notes that what is often labelled the 'fear of success' is in reality a fear of *subsequent* failure. A socially anxious individual, for example, may fear that overcoming her anxiety (and its associated avoidance behaviour) could lead her into social situations in which failure (that is, rejection by others) may be a very real possibility. She therefore is actually afraid of failing socially, rather than fearing that she will be successful. When Ellis encounters resistance related to the fear of change or the 'fear of success', he looks for irrational beliefs such as 'I *must not* give up my symptoms, as change would be *too* uncomfortable' or 'I *must* remain disturbed, since becoming less disturbed and doing better in life might expose me to *awful* failures (which I absolutely *couldn't stand*) later on.' By helping clients to dispute and surrender these beliefs, he is often able to minimize these forms of resistance within therapy.

Resistance Motivated by Reactance and Rebelliousness. Some clients, even though they have sought therapy voluntarily, resist the therapist's ministrations because they view them as an infringement of their freedom. This form of resistance may particularly be encountered in active-directive therapies such as REBT (Ellis, 1985c, 1990b). Ellis notes that it can be underpinned by irrational beliefs such as: 'I *have to* control my entire destiny; even though my therapist is on my side and is working hard to help me, I *must not* allow him or her to tell me what to do! It's *awful* to be directed by my therapist, and I *can't bear it*! I *should* be free to think and act in my usual ways, even if my symptoms are self-defeating!' As with other types of resistance outlined above, Ellis helps clients to recognize and dispute the irrational beliefs behind their rebelliousness within therapy. He also notes that he and other rational emotive behaviour therapists may sometimes selectively employ paradoxical intention in order to help clients to think, act and emote in less self-defeating ways (Ellis, 1985c, 1990b). Paradoxical techniques, however, are generally not emphasized within REBT by Ellis because they can shift the focus away from assisting clients to develop more rational philosophies of life.

As the foregoing material suggests, Ellis places an emphasis upon cognitive methods with respect to helping resistant clients. He is opposed, however, to the compulsive overuse of one favoured method at the expense of others that may also prove beneficial. Thus, he will also employ emotive and behavioural techniques in the service of overcoming resistance. He notes that with highly resistant individuals, it can be particularly important to attack their resistance-producing irrational beliefs in a very comprehensive and thoroughgoing manner.

Ellis's Views on Therapists' Problems

In his writings on resistance, Ellis (1985c, 1990b) identifies a wide variety of irrational beliefs – held by clients and/or therapists – that can impede the process of therapy. He has also written about several irrational beliefs to which mental health practitioners may be prone to subscribe (Ellis, 1984b). When these beliefs are in operation, they can lead to therapeutic inefficiency and make counsellors and therapists vulnerable to significant emotional upsets. These irrational beliefs, along with their corollaries, are as follows:

1 I *have to* be successful with all of my clients practically all of the time.
   (a) I must continually make brilliant and profound interpretations.
   (b) I must always have good judgement.
   (c) I must help my clients *more* than I am now helping them.
   (d) If I fail with any of my clients, it has to be my fault.
   (e) When I fail, as I must not, I'm a thoroughly lousy therapist – and a rotten person!
   (f) My successes don't count if I have a *real* failure.
2 I *must* be an outstanding therapist, clearly better than other therapists I know or hear about.
   (a) I must succeed even with impossible clients.
   (b) I must have *all* good sessions with my clients.
   (c) I must use the greatest and most prestigious system of therapy and be outstanding at using it.
   (d) I must be famous as a therapist.
   (e) Because I am a therapist, I should have no emotional problems myself and am disgraced if I do.
3 I *have to* be greatly respected and loved by all my clients.
   (a) I must not dislike any of my clients and especially must not show that I dislike them.
   (b) I must not push my clients too hard, lest they then hate me.
   (c) I must avoid ticklish issues that might upset and antagonize my clients.

(d) The clients whom I like and who like me must remain in therapy practically forever.

(e) My clients must see that I am thoroughly devoted to them and that I never make any mistakes.

(f) It's horrible to be disapproved of by any of my clients because their disapproval makes me a bad therapist and a rotten person.

4 Since I am doing my best and working so hard as a therapist, my clients *should* be equally hardworking and responsible, *should* listen to me carefully, and *should* always push themselves to change.

(a) My clients should not be difficult and resistant!

(b) They should do exactly what I tell them to do!

(c) They should work very hard in between sessions and always do their therapeutic homework!

(d) I should only have young, bright, attractive and not too difficult clients.

5 Because I am a person in my own right, I *must* be able to enjoy myself during therapy sessions and to use these sessions to solve my personal problems as much as to help clients with their difficulties.

(a) I must mainly use therapeutic techniques that I enjoy using, whether or not they are very helpful to clients.

(b) I must only use techniques that are easy and do not wear me out.

(c) I must make considerable money doing therapy and must not have to work too hard to make it.

(d) If I exploit some of my clients amatively and sexually, that will do both them and me a lot of good.

(e) Because I am so helpful as a therapist, I should be able to get away with coming late to appointments, cancelling them at the last minute, sleeping during sessions, and indulging myself in other ways.

Ellis notes that therapists may be resistant to working to overcome their own irrational beliefs, and cites these factors as contributing to this resistance:

first, you may be reluctant to admit that you, a psychotherapist, really have deep-seated emotional difficulties. Second, you may be so preoccupied with helping others that you rarely think about helping yourself. Third, you may wrongly assume that your authoritative knowledge of disturbance and your self-explorations during your training protect you from being disturbed about the therapeutic process. Fourth, you may have the same kind of low frustration tolerance –

commonly known as laziness – that prevents many of your own clients from working to change themselves. Fifth, you may be so involved with yourself that you myopically fail to see shortcomings and emotional difficulties that a more objective observer would observe. (Ellis, 1984b: 30)

Ellis (1984b) encourages therapists and counsellors to work concertedly at identifying the irrational beliefs that interfere with their therapeutic effectiveness, and to employ a comprehensive assortment of REBT techniques in the service of disputing them. He suggests that therapists and counsellors first attempt to work on their emotional and behavioural problems independently without the assistance of a mental health practitioner, so that they might be better able to appreciate the struggles of their own clients as they attempt to achieve self-change.

Having reviewed Ellis's major contributions to theory and practice within the fields of counselling and psychotherapy, we turn now to consideration of some of the major criticisms to which his ideas and his approach to clinical practice have been subjected. As the reader will soon see, Ellis and REBT have been criticized on many different dimensions by a veritable host of writers. Chapter 4 begins by reviewing some of the reasons that Ellis and REBT have received such an abundance of critical attention, and then presents criticisms and rebuttals in six important areas.

4

Criticisms and Rebuttals

In considering the highly emotionalized objections that are often
raised against rational-emotive principles and procedures by
sundry adherents of different schools, it would be easy to say
'That's their problem!' and let it go at that ... It is also,
however, very much *our* problem if some of the objections
raised to rational-emotive procedures are valid ... [Let us,]
therefore, consider some of the most cogent and relevant
protests that have been raised against [REBT] and try to answer
them with a minimum of irrational evasiveness or hostility.

(Ellis, 1962: 331)

Overview

Albert Ellis's formulations of rational emotive behavioural theory
and therapy have been subjected to critical examination by a
veritable legion of writers. Why have Ellis and REBT been critiqued
so thoroughly? There are probably three main factors that account
for this phenomenon.

First, Ellis is a prolific writer. To date, he has put forward his
ideas on the theory and practice of effective psychotherapy in scores
of books, monographs and professional papers. In addition, he has
given many hundreds of lectures and workshops on REBT. Such
exposure does not, of course, guarantee that one's ideas will receive
critical attention, but it may very well increase the likelihood that
this will occur.

Second, many of Ellis's ideas on psychotherapy theory and
practice have been quite controversial. His position that psychoanalysis and client-centred therapy are relatively ineffective and
inefficient forms of treatment, for example, runs counter to the
cherished beliefs of a substantial number of professionals within the
therapeutic community. His strong views on the biological basis of
irrational thinking in humans have also run in opposition to
prevalent environmentalist theories of human behaviour and

personality. In addition, his theory concerning a link between religiosity and emotional disturbance has stimulated a flurry of critical (and, at times emotional) responses.

Finally, Ellis's manner of presenting his views to lay and professional audiences has drawn him a good deal of (sometimes negative) attention. He is no shrinking violet, by any means. He openly speaks his mind on topics that are of interest to him, and will not hesitate to label as 'horseshit' any ideas concerning therapy that he views as illogical or unscientific. Profane language is not uncommon during an Albert Ellis workshop or lecture. Also, Ellis makes statements that some professionals may regard as flamboyant or outlandish (for example, 'Freud was born with a gene for inefficiency, while I was born with a gene for efficiency!'). The attention that he receives is certainly not unwelcome to him; Ellis developed his particular public speaking style in order to increase his impact on his audiences.

In this chapter we attempt to outline briefly some of the major criticisms that have been levelled against Ellis and REBT. Each criticism presented receives a rebuttal, based mainly upon Ellis's writings. We would like the reader to note that the review we present in this chapter should not be regarded as absolutely complete; some of the more minor points upon which Ellis and REBT have been critiqued (as well as criticisms that have been based on obviously incorrect information) have been omitted. We present critiques concerning (a) Ellis's practice of REBT, (b) goals and values espoused in REBT, (c) REBT's theoretical tenets (including Ellis's theory regarding the biographical basis of irrational thinking), (d) REBT and religion, (e) REBT, rationalism and constructivism and (d) research support for REBT's clinical efficacy.

Ellis's Practice of REBT

Criticisms
The manner in which Ellis actually practises REBT has received critical scrutiny from a number of writers. Some of these individuals have been critical of Ellis for 'fitting the client to the therapy', regardless of the problems to receive therapeutic attention. Meichenbaum (1979), for instance, has referred to Ellis and REBT as seducing, cajoling and teaching clients to view their maladaptive feelings and behaviour within the ABC framework. Dolliver (1979) has noted his puzzlement over the fact that although Ellis (1950, 1974) has criticized both psychoanalysis and Janov's primal therapy for 'training' clients to find evidence in

support of the accuracy of particular therapeutic hypotheses (for example, present-day adult problems have their roots in childhood trauma), he has nevertheless stated that:

> [The rational therapist] knows, even before he talks to the client, that this client *must* believe some silly, irrational ideas – otherwise he/she could not possibly be disturbed. And, knowing this, the rational therapist deliberately looks for these irrationalities, often predicts them, and soon discovers and explains them. (Ellis, 1957a: 41)

Dolliver (1979: 214) goes on to state that 'Movies and tapes of Ellis doing RET give ample evidence that Ellis promotes the client's buying into an RET view of psychological processes.' Comments and criticisms such as these portray Ellis as an authoritarian therapist and REBT as a Procrustean approach to treatment.

In a related vein, A.A. Lazarus (1989), the creator of Multimodal Therapy, has noted that he has seen many clients in therapy who did not appear to subscribe to any of the specific irrational beliefs that Ellis (1962; Ellis and Harper, 1975) has identified in his writings. Rather, their problems seemed to be related to other sorts of cognitions such as 'happiness is dangerous; let your anger out; the less personal information you disclose, the better off you will be; it is generally good to show that you are right; total self-sufficiency is attainable and desirable' (Lazarus, 1989: 100). Lazarus (1989: 100) indicates that in his view Ellis and REBT tend to 'employ Procrustean maneuvers – fitting the client to 11 or 12 preconceived beliefs'.

Ellis and REBT have also been criticized for placing too much emphasis upon cognitive disputing. Lazarus (1979, 1989) has been particularly vocal with respect to this issue. He has made the observation, for example, that

> After listening to many of Ellis's therapy tapes, seeing several of his films and videos, and perusing a good deal of the literature on rational-emotive procedures, it seems to me that disputation is employed about 90% of the time. With few exceptions, it would appear that most RET practitioners seldom use methods outside of actively explaining, interpreting, and disputing clients' irrational beliefs. (Lazarus, 1989: 98)

Lazarus (1989) expresses the view that Ellis and other rational emotive behaviour therapists may tend to under-utilize other sorts of techniques that could be potentially helpful to clients, such as paradoxical interventions and imagery methods.

Ellis has also received criticism for his use of profanity within therapy sessions and for adopting what is sometimes perceived as an overly confrontational stance with clients. I (J.Y.) have talked with a number of laypeople and mental health professionals who, after attending one of Ellis's public demonstrations of REBT (such as at his regular Friday evening workshop, 'Problems of Daily Living', at the Institute for Rational-Emotive Therapy in New York City), voiced negative reactions. Some of these individuals expressed the belief that obscene language is simply inappropriate within the context of psychotherapy. A number of laypersons stated their view that they could not feel comfortable and be fully self-disclosing with a therapist who comes across in such a strongly confrontational manner. Some mental health practitioners indicated their belief that Ellis pokes fun at his clients and that strong confrontation is likely to be harmful for certain individuals. These 'critics' all seem to hold the view that Ellis's therapeutic style is actually anti-therapeutic.

Rebuttals

With respect to Meichenbaum's (1979) charge that Ellis and REBT seduce, cajole and teach clients to view their problems within the ABC framework, Ellis has responded by stating that

> *This* is what the RET therapist 'seduces, cajoles, and teaches' most clients to do – to think for themselves, to learn the scientific method and to actively use it for the rest of their lives, and thereby to make themselves less conditionable, less reinforceable, and less suggestible to external stimuli, including social approval. (1979f: 250)

Ellis would certainly acknowledge his role as *teacher* in his therapeutic work, but his position is that he is teaching clients the means to critically examine their thinking such that they are able to identify and challenge the cognitions that lead them into emotional disturbance. Ellis's teaching style can be characterized as *authoritative* but not *authoritarian*, as he does not absolutistically insist that clients learn and utilize the philosophical disputing techniques that he attempts to convey to them.

Ellis (1979f) acknowledges that the quote cited by Dolliver (1979) – that the rational emotive behaviour therapist 'knows . . . that this client *must* believe some silly, irrational ideas' – is dogmatically overstated, and that he would no longer subscribe to it. He has, in fact, qualified and modified this quote so that it is less absolutistic and more probabilistic in tone:

> The RET practitioner knows on *theoretical grounds*, even before he talks to the client, that his client *most probably* has some silly, irrational ideas – particularly, that he holds some absolutistic shoulds and musts – otherwise he would *very likely* not be disturbed. And, knowing this, the rational therapist deliberately looks for these irrationalities, often predicts them, and *most often* is able to discover them, to get the client to agree that they exist, and to show the client how to logico-empirically dispute and surrender them. (Ellis, 1979f: 252–3; emphasis added)

In terms of Dolliver's (1979) observation that he 'promotes the client's buying into an RET view of psychological processes', Ellis (1979f: 253) responds by iterating that what he is 'selling' is the 'scientific method of looking at one's own hypotheses or assumptions and questioning and challenging them'. Ellis claims that primal therapists and psychoanalysts teach clients to be even more gullible than they already are, and makes the point that a 'therapist's "selling" gullibility and "selling" a logico-empirical, problem-solving method of thinking are quite different kinds of "salesmanship"!' (1979f: 253).

Ellis has not offered a response to A.A. Lazarus's (1989) observation that many clients do not seem to subscribe to any of the specific irrational beliefs delineated in his writings (Ellis, 1962; Ellis and Harper, 1975). It is interesting to speculate, however, that some of the alternative disturbance-producing beliefs posited by Lazarus may actually have particular musts and shoulds underlying them. Take, for example, the attitude that 'the less personal information you disclose, the better off you will be'. A rational emotive behaviour therapist, working with a client who has revealed that he holds this attitude, may find upon further exploration that it stems from the following irrational belief: 'I *must* never reveal things about myself that might cause me to be rejected by other people, because rejection is *awful* and would prove that I'm a thoroughly worthless human being.' It may be the case that Lazarus (1989) fails to find musts and shoulds in his clients' thinking because he is specifically looking for some of the eleven or twelve major irrational beliefs originally outlined by Ellis (1962; Ellis and Harper, 1975) in some of his earlier writings. Contemporary rational emotive behaviour therapists are able to exercise a greater degree of fluidity as they search for clients' irrational beliefs, as they don't confine themselves to an itemized list. Rather, following Ellis's more current model, they more broadly look for absolutistic demands directed at the self, other people or conditions in the world (Ellis and Bernard, 1985; Ellis and Dryden, 1987). They recognize that human beings are capable of manufacturing musts and shoulds of an almost infinite variety.

With respect to Lazarus's (1989) criticism that cognitive disputing is overemphasized by Ellis and other REBT practitioners, Ellis (1989c) acknowledges that REBT favours methods that will help clients to make a profound philosophic change in the irrational beliefs that underpin their emotional and behavioural problems. Rational emotive behaviour therapists will usually attempt to employ philosophical disputing with many (if not most) clients, as this is viewed as the most effective means of overcoming present and avoiding future disturbances. They will, however, employ other methods if it appears that philosophical disputing is not benefiting particular clients. Thus, Ellis (1989c) takes issue with Lazarus's (1989) comment that most REBT practitioners rarely employ any other procedures in their clinical work. He notes that survey research conducted by Warren and McLellarn (1987) revealed that REBT practitioners will frequently utilize 'unconditional acceptance of clients, strong forceful language, social skills training, role playing, behavior rehearsal, rational-emotive imagery, modeling, problem-solving training, contingency contracting, and other nondisputing techniques' (Ellis, 1989c: 219). Ellis promotes using a variety of procedures for facilitating profound philosophical change, and advocates a host of other techniques if it seems that change on this level does not appear feasible.

With respect to the charge that Ellis and other rational emotive behaviour therapists may tend to under-utilize certain methods such as imagery techniques and paradoxical interventions (Lazarus, 1989), Ellis (1985c, 1989c) has expressed doubts as to just how helpful these methods really are to clients. As noted in Chapter 3, Ellis (1982, 1984e) is concerned that a good number of commonly used therapeutic techniques may serve to sidetrack clients from the important task of examining their upset-producing ideas. He has noted that many imagery techniques are generally by-passed by REBT therapists because there are few controlled studies backing their effectiveness (Ellis, 1989c). With reference to techniques such as paradoxical intention, Ellis (1985c: 159) has written that 'Unusually clever and unique methods . . . had better remain just that – unusual and unique. Run of the mill cognitive, emotive and behavioral techniques that can be used with many clients much of the time will probably prove more economical and useful.'

Ellis has defended his use of profanity in therapy sessions against critics who believe that such language is inappropriate within the context of psychotherapy. He believes that 'the sprightly use of obscenity' (Ellis, 1977a) can serve as a vehicle for emphasizing particular points that he wishes to make to clients, and that it can also function as a vehicle for breaking down some of the barriers to intimacy that can exist between client and therapist. Wiener (1988: 8), writing in his biography of Ellis, has stated that Ellis claims that 'everyone thinks in such language, even if not talking that way', and that he believes that 'it liberates audiences and clients to have him release these suppressed words that they presumably often use at least silently, in their heads'. It is noted, however, that Ellis does not employ profanity injudiciously in his therapeutic work. Review of audiotapes of his clinical sessions reveals that his use of strong language varies from client to client (Yankura and Dryden, 1990). As with other therapeutic tools, Ellis will modify or even abandon his use of profanity if it appears that it prompts negative reactions in a given client.

With respect to criticism that he is overly confrontational with clients, Ellis (1985c) believes that comparatively strong confrontation can help to make therapy more effective and efficient, particularly with many difficult and resistant clients. As noted in Chapter 3, he advises therapists to be cautious about providing an overabundance of warmth and love to their clients (Ellis, 1982, 1991c). In his view this can become an impediment to effective treatment, as it may serve to reinforce clients' beliefs that they absolutely *need* the love and approval of significant others. In addition, Ellis (Hoellen and Ellis, 1986) has made the observation that overly warm therapists may tend to gloss over their clients' errors and negative characteristics, with the result that they refrain from engaging in potentially helpful therapeutic activities such as forceful disputing of irrational beliefs and keeping after clients who continually 'goof off' with respect to their homework assignments. As far as poking fun at clients is concerned, the authors of this volume have never observed this behaviour at any of Ellis's public demonstrations of REBT nor heard it in reviewing audiotapes of his therapy sessions. Ellis (1977a) may lampoon clients' irrational beliefs in order to highlight their illogical and unhelpful aspects, but he does not put down or make fun of his clients. As stated in earlier chapters, he is, in fact, a strong advocate of providing clients with unconditional acceptance.

Goals and Values Espoused in REBT

Criticisms

Laypeople and mental health professionals alike have sometimes criticized REBT in terms of the goals (or values) they believe it foists upon clients. Mahoney, Lyddon and Alford (1989), for instance, in their review of the REBT theory of psychotherapy, present the view that REBT pushes clients towards apathy, resignation, and detachment with respect to unfortunate life experiences. They state that:

> The message is clear. Echoing the ideas of Epictetus, Ellis invites us to recognize what little control we have over our lives, to renounce any hope of supernatural meaning or salvation, and to accept our lives as they are. (There is a modern bumper sticker that conveys the same basic outlook: 'Life sucks, and then you die.') We cannot change the reality of our slavery (literal or symbolic), but we can change what we demand of

life and we can aim toward a rational detachment that will ease our pain. (Mahoney, Lyddon and Alford, 1989: 92)

This perception of Ellis and REBT is based upon these authors' knowledge that Ellis's formulation of the principles of REBT was influenced in part by the thinking of some of the ancient Greek Stoic philosophers (particularly Epictetus, a slave) and probably also by the fact that Ellis generally encourages clients to recognize that unfortunate activating events are not *awful* and that they *can* stand them.

In a related vein, Dryden and Gordon (1990) have noted that REBT has occasionally been criticized for encouraging clients to become unfeeling robots. Lazarus (1989: 106) has expressed the observation that the goal of Ellis's 'preferential' REBT appears to be 'to achieve a state of veritable undisturbability (rather than merely striving to be less disturbable)'. Such criticisms and observations seem to emanate from a perspective in which REBT is viewed as being absolutely opposed to negative emotions of all sorts. Critics rightly observe that an existence in which negative emotions are never experienced would be rather flat and dull, as well as being next to impossible for most human beings to achieve.

On another dimension, Woolfolk and Sass (1989) find flaws in Ellis's espousal of enlightened self-interest and long-range hedonism as components of good psychological health. In offering their critique, they cite the following passage from Ellis's (1973a: 159) own writings:

> The emotionally healthy individual is primarily true to himself and does not masochistically sacrifice himself for others. His kindness and consideration for others are largely derived from the idea that he himself wants to enjoy freedom from unnecessary pain and restriction, and that he is only likely to do so by helping create a world in which the rights of others, as well as his own rights, are not needlessly curtailed.

Woolfolk and Sass (1989) criticize Ellis for apparently espousing a view in which human beings treat others well simply because they find this to be the best mechanism for getting their own needs met – altruistic behaviour thus becomes a means to an end, rather than an end in itself. Also, with respect to the REBT goal of long-range hedonism, Woolfolk and Sass (1989: 23) make the observation that 'If one is fundamentally and primarily for oneself, it would seem that, on assessing long-term prospects for satisfaction, one might just as well resolve to become a very effective psychopath as choose to fashion oneself into an altruistic social democrat.' The points that these authors raise are important ones, for if Ellis and REBT are indeed teaching individuals to be self-centred mavericks, the case could be made that REBT clients are 'benefiting' from treatment at a potentially great expense to the larger social community.

Rebuttals

In responding to Mahoney, Lyddon and Alford's (1989) claim that REBT pushes clients toward apathy and resignation, Ellis (1989c) has first indicated that while his thinking has been influenced by the writings of Epictetus, he has hardly accepted all of this ancient Stoic philosopher's ideas:

> [Epictetus] believed in inalterable fate; he did not usually advocate changing obnoxious conditions that can be changed; he was utopian; he downplayed human emotion and pleasure; he advocated calmness, serenity, and detachment; and he had many other ideas that are quite antithetical to RET. The main ideas I took from him (and from some of the early Asian philosophers as well) are, first, that it is not things but largely (not completely!) our view of things that upsets us; and, second, that if we profoundly change our self-upsetting view we can significantly help change our dysfunctional feelings and behaviors. (1989c: 215)

Ellis goes on to state that,

> I clearly keep saying that we have much control over our lives and that we have only to accept things as they are after we have made concerted efforts to change them and have found these efforts useless. Even then, I keep emphasizing to my clients that they had better only temporarily accept unfortunate events and relationships that they cannot change, and had better virtually never give up the ultimate hope of changing them. (1989c: 215)

In point of fact, it appears that Ellis never encourages his clients to surrender to 'inalterable fate'; rather, within his therapy sessions, he constantly encourages (and even at times pushes) them to take constructive action – either to challenge their upset-producing irrational beliefs, or to modify the unfortunate activating events in their lives. It must be said, however, that even when he encourages clients to work at changing some of the negative circumstances of their lives, he also concurrently tries to show them how not to upset themselves about these circumstances as long as they are in existence. In many respects, Ellis's approach is encompassed in the well-known *Serenity Prayer*: 'Grant me the serenity to accept the things I cannot change/The ability to change the things I can change/And the wisdom to know the difference.'

Ellis (1989c) strongly takes issue with Lazarus's (1989) contention that the goal of preferential REBT is to achieve a state of veritable undisturbability for clients. He notes that for many years he has espoused the position that virtually all human beings seem to have inborn tendencies to make themselves disturbed, and that even clients who have been significantly helped by REBT may still sometimes temporarily fall back to disturbance (Ellis, 1976a, 1989c). Such clients may, however, fall back less frequently and recover more quickly when they do create upsets for themselves.

In addition, Ellis does not regard all types of negative feelings as being unhealthy and neurotic, and he doesn't set himself the therapeutic goal of attempting to help clients do away with all forms of negative emotion. As described in Chapter 2, Ellis differentiates between *unhealthy* and *healthy* negative emotions (Ellis, 1973a, 1977b, 1980c). Unhealthy negative emotions (including anxiety, depression, anger, guilt and shame) are very extreme responses to unfortunate activating events (stemming from particular irrational beliefs held by the individual), and will usually (although not always) contribute to self-defeating behavioural consequences. Healthy negative emotions (such as annoyance, concern, regret, disappointment and sadness) tend to be more reasonable responses to unfortunate activating events (and stem from not having one's personally meaningful wants and preferences met), and will most often not lead to self-defeating behavioural consequences. *Healthy* negative emotions are valued in REBT because they can function as an important source of motivation for attempts to modify undesirable life conditions. In responding to the criticism that REBT encourages clients to become unfeeling robots, Dryden and Gordon have written the following:

> When clients are faced with negative life events, such as the loss of loved ones, RET therapists encourage such clients to feel keenly appropriate emotions, such as sorrow, sadness, and grief. An emotion-free existence, even if it could be achieved, has no place in the RET view of things. Such an existence would seem a very dull, sterile sort of state in which to 'live' and could only be achieved by the abandonment of all desire and the creation of an attitude of total indifference to the world. That would be, indeed, the exact opposite of the RET philosophy, and no good RET therapist would ever attempt to do any such thing. (1990: 102)

In addressing the criticisms of his views on self interest and long-range hedonism made by Woolfolk and Sass (1989), Ellis (1989c) first acknowledges that REBT holds that one of the *main* reasons for acting ethically and altruistically is because such behaviour may well help to create a world in which others will act in a similar fashion toward you. He goes on to state, however, that REBT also recognizes that individuals can choose to be kind, considerate or loving simply because they *prefer* to act in these ways and derive pleasure from doing so. Ellis (1989c) believes (along with many other psychologists and philosophers) that such things as generosity, altruism and love are tendencies that are partly innate to human beings, and that they are not merely learned or figured out by individuals who are driven exclusively by self-interest. With respect to the criticism that a focus on self-interest and long-range hedonism may encourage some individuals to become 'very effective psychopaths', Ellis (1989c) points out that psychopaths typically go for short-term rather than long-term satisfaction, and that they are often caught and penalized for choosing actions that violate society's rules and the rights of others. He also notes that they sabotage the larger social group through their psychopathic behaviours, 'and thereby, in the short and long run, tend to live more miserably themselves' (Ellis, 1989c: 201). In fact, when working with psychopathic clients, Ellis (1962, 1985c) has indicated that after establishing rapport with them he determinedly attempts to show them that their unethical and anti-social acts are very likely going to result in *self*-defeating consequences.

REBT's Basic Theoretical Tenets

Criticisms

A number of writers have criticized REBT's ABC model as being too simplistic a representation of the relationships between thoughts, feelings and behaviours (Meichenbaum, 1979; Mahoney, Lyddon and Alford, 1989). These critics maintain that Ellis and REBT downplay or ignore the complex interactions of these three major dimensions of human psychological functioning. Schwartz (1984) has advanced that REBT should be regarded as a cognitive primacy theory (as opposed to an interactionist theory) of personality and human change processes, as it largely focuses upon cognition as having a causal or mediating role with respect to the affective, behavioural and physiological domains. In fact, Schwartz (1984) notes that in a comprehensive review of empirical support for REBT's clinical theory, Ellis (1977f) fails to advance a single specific hypothesis delineating a causal role for either affect or behaviour in human psychological functioning. Schwartz (1984) and Mahoney, Lyddon and Alford (1989) see more recent accounts of REBT theory as attempting to place a greater emphasis on the interdependent and interactive nature of cognition, emotion and behaviour; nevertheless, they still contend that REBT's focus is clearly cognitive in both theory and practice. In support of this view, they cite the following passage by Dryden and Ellis:

> A model which emphasizes the interactive and interdependent nature of intrapsychic and interpersonal processes does not have to take the position that all have equal explanatory variance in accounting for human psychological disturbance. Indeed, RET has become renowned

for the central role it has given to cognition in general and to evaluative beliefs in particular in its theory and practice. (1988: 218)

Although this is not clearly stated, Mahoney, Lyddon and Alford (1989) seem to imply that a system of psychotherapy that gives so much emphasis to cognition will be significantly limited with respect to its capacity to promote human psychological growth and personality change.

Mahoney, Lyddon and Alford (1989: 85) also suggest that REBT theory 'reflects a very basic, *formistic* thinking style'. They describe formistic thinking (after Pepper, 1942) as 'essentially categorical in nature; things and events are classified in a binary, either–or fashion'. In the view of these authors, REBT oversimplifies the phenomena of cognitions and emotions by describing them in two distinct categories. Thoughts can be either rational or irrational, and feelings can be either positive or negative. Such dichotomous classes, they claim, are actually similar to some of the types of cognitive errors challenged within REBT.

Rebuttals

In responding to critics (Meichenbaum, 1979; Schwartz, 1984; Mahoney, Lyddon and Alford, 1989) who state that REBT is a cognitive primacy theory and that its ABC model oversimplifies the complex inter-relationships between thoughts, feelings and behaviours, Ellis (1989c) acknowledges that REBT (like other forms of cognitive-behavioural therapy) has not yet developed a detailed theory as to how emotions and behaviours may influence thinking processes. He indicates that REBT nevertheless recognizes that such relationships very probably exist and that they can have relevance to the process of psychotherapy. Ellis (1962, 1984d, 1989c) and REBT, however, *do* view irrational beliefs as largely (but not completely) 'creating' emotional and behavioural disturbances. In explaining his emphasis upon identifying and disputing clients' irrational beliefs within therapy, Ellis has offered the following statement:

> I stated in 1961 that cognitive, emotive and behavioral processes all significantly interact and that emotion and action affect thinking, as well as the latter influences the former. But I do believe that humans, unlike lower animals, *more* profoundly, *more* pervasively, *more* importantly change their emotions and actions by changing their thinking than they modify their thoughts by changing their emotions or behaviors. (1979f: 261)

Despite this position, he strongly holds that REBT is an interactive approach and should not be placed in the cognitive primacy fold. In a response to Schwartz's (1982) paper which categorizes REBT as a cognitive primacy approach, Ellis stated that:

> [RET] contends that if [humans] are to achieve *elegant* and *lasting* personality changes they had better become quite conscious of their irrational beliefs and keep working at changing them (Ellis, 1979c, 1979f, 1980c). But it also theorizes that because humans are innately predisposed to think, emote, and behave interactionally, and virtually never disparately, they rarely make and sustain fundamental cognitive changes unless they consistently (and also uncomfortably) practice, practice, and practice new behaviors. RET – which is not idly named rational-*emotive* therapy – therefore stresses cognitive, affective, and behavioral techniques . . . (Ellis, 1984f: 217)

REBT's interactionist stance is perhaps most clearly expressed in its actual clinical applications with clients. Cognitive techniques (such as philosophical disputing and the use of rational self-statements), for example, may be used to help clients make changes in their disordered feelings and behaviour; emotive and behavioural methods are employed to help clients modify their self-defeating ideas. It is also worthwhile noting that Ellis (1989c) has indicated that somewhat simplistic 'causative' relationships (for example, irrational beliefs 'cause' unhealthy negative emotions) may be stressed to clients during a course of rational emotive behaviour therapy in order to increase their motivation to work hard at modifying their irrational beliefs and dysfunctional feelings.

As an added historical footnote, the reader is reminded that Ellis changed the name of his approach from *rational* therapy to rational-*emotive* therapy in order to correct the misconceptions that (a) he was a proponent of rationalist philosophy, and (b) his method tended to ignore feelings. At a 1993 conference on integrating cognitive-behavioural and psychoanalytic approaches to treatment, Ellis made a public announcement that he was again changing the name of the therapy – this time, to rational emotive *behaviour* therapy. It seems clear that this announcement represented a further attempt on Ellis's part to counter the notion that his approach over-focuses on cognition and the utilization of cognitive techniques.

Finally, with specific reference to the criticism that REBT's ABC model is too simplistic, it is noted that Ellis (1991b) has recently published a revised version of the ABC's of rational emotive behaviour therapy. His paper details numerous complex inter-relationships of A's, B's and C's, such as how A's can influence B's, B's can influence A's, C's can influence B's and so on. He also offers an updated version of the ABC's of disturbed interpersonal relationships. While a detailed explication of the content of this paper is beyond the scope of this chapter, it is recommended reading for any practitioner wishing to be up to date on Ellis's views concerning the interactional nature of human psychological processes.

With respect to the criticism that REBT describes complex psychological phenomena such as cognitions and emotions in terms of simplistic, dichotomous categories (Mahoney, Lyddon and Alford, 1989), Ellis has responded by indicating that this is simply not the case:

> RET separates thoughts into (a) rational thoughts (preferences, wishes, desires, wants), (b) irrational thoughts (antiempirical and illogical ideas) that do not necessarily create disturbances (e.g. beliefs in gods and devils), and (c) irrational thoughts (dogmatic, imperative, and musturbatory ideas) that very frequently (though not necessarily) do contribute significantly to disturbances. RET separates emotions into (a) positive emotions that are self-helpful, (b) positive emotions that are often self-sabotaging, (c) negative feelings that are functional and desirable, (d) negative feelings that are dysfunctional and self-defeating ... (1989c: 213–14)

In addition to the above distinctions, it is also noted that REBT discriminates between non-evaluative and evaluative thoughts (for example, inferences versus irrational beliefs) and holds that both rational and irrational beliefs can vary with respect to the intensity with which they are held by individuals (Dryden and Yankura, 1993). Thus, in many respects, it appears that REBT makes finer discriminations with regard to its conceptualizations of human thinking and emoting than do many of the other forms of cognitive-behavioural therapy currently practised.

Ellis's Theory on the Biological Basis of Irrational Thinking in Humans

Criticisms

During the mid-1950s, when Ellis was first formulating and presenting his views on REBT, he leaned toward an environmentalist view with respect to the origins of human psychological disturbance (Dryden, 1990b). In other words, he tended to hold the position, still prevalent within the psychotherapeutic community, that cultural and familial factors were largely responsible for the development of 'neurosis'. As he gained experience as a therapist, however, he encountered an increasing amount of evidence that suggested to him that almost all severely neurotic, borderline and psychotic individuals had a strong innate tendency to cognitively exaggerate environmental stresses and thus disturb themselves. He continued to develop his views in this regard and presented them in a paper entitled, 'The biological basis of human irrationality' (1976a). His position on the respective contributions of nature versus nurture in human psychological functioning is summarized in the following quote:

> Although almost all contemporary schools of psychotherapy and personality formation take a different view, it seems probable that the main influence on human personality comes from hereditary sources . . . my RET-oriented theory of personality says that probably 80% of the variance in human behavior rests largely on biological bases and 20% or so on specific environmental training. (Ellis, 1979g: 17)

This is a strong statement to make, and it is at variance with the positions held by some of the other major schools of psychotherapy. Thus, it is not surprising that Ellis's views on this issue have received critical scrutiny in a number of different ways.

Ziegler (1989: 35) notes that given Ellis's strong leanings toward constitutionalism, 'a present glaring omission in RET theory is a careful, systematic, and detailed account of the origin of irrational (and rational) beliefs in terms that are compatible with and, if possible, grounded in the known facts of genetics and neuroscience'. Other writers (for example, Eschenroeder, 1982) have criticized Ellis and REBT for not systematically taking into account how environmental influences may contribute to individuals' formation of and adherence to irrational beliefs.

Taking a somewhat different tack with their critique of Ellis's 1976a paper, McBurnett and LaPointe (1978) attempt to point out some illogicalities in Ellis's contention that self-defeating emotional and behavioural consequences are the result of humans' innate irrationality . They indicate, for instance, that 'for any goal, there is only one most efficient available means of attainment and a plethora of more stupid means. From a strictly statistical standpoint, the probability of occurrence of a given rational behaviour is extremely low' (McBurnett and LaPointe, 1978: 202). They argue that self-defeating human errors can be adequately explained with reference to task complexity (that is, the demands of discerning and acting upon the most rational choice for a given problematic situation), and that there is thus no need to invoke a biological explanation for such errors.

Rebuttals

Ellis (1989c) concurs with Ziegler's observation that REBT theory lacks a detailed account, based in genetics and neuroscience, of the origin of irrational and rational beliefs. To date, such an account has still not been presented. It is noted, however, that aspects of Ellis's theory on the biological basis of human irrationality are receiving attention from and being further developed by other rational emotive behaviour theorists. Ruth (1992), for instance, has offered an evolutionary proposal for Ellis's genetic postulate for irrational thinking in humans. He hypothesizes that 'a genetic potential for irrational thinking may have evolved in humans due to an ability to facilitate adaptive behaviours and emotions in the interest of securing critical advantages in early childhood development, increased reproductive success, and basic survival' (Ruth, 1992: 17). As an example (with reference to the issue of reproductive success), Ruth states that

> if [a primitive] individual believes that one 'must' and 'should' mate, that one absolutely 'needs' to address this urge, and that one 'deserves' and is 'entitled' to complete fulfillment, then this individual would probably feel more compelled and lustful, and engage in sexually related behaviors and strategies more readily, than another individual who did not believe, or believed less, in such ideas. (1992: 13)

He notes that while the potential for irrational thinking may still have adaptive value for children at earlier stages of development (insofar as absolutistic demandingness may contribute to basic need fulfilment by caretakers), it is questionable whether it serves any useful function for adults who are presumably more capable of 'higher-order thinking and mature responsiveness'. The notion that irrational thinking strongly and often contributes to self-defeating consequences for adults is, of course, in accordance with Ellis's own theories.

With respect to the criticism that he has failed to detail how environmental influences contribute to the development and maintenance of irrational beliefs, it is important to bear in mind that Ellis (1979g) holds that 'probably 80% of the variance in human behavior rests largely on biological bases . . .'. Thus, as suggested by Ziegler (1989: 36), it may be the case that 'Ellis's strong constitutionalist leanings lead him to downplay, relatively speaking, careful attention to potentially important specific environmental influences in personality development'. Ellis (1989c) acknowledges that there may be some truth in this statement, but stresses that as a psychotherapist he is mainly interested in personality *change*, as opposed to personality development. As he has stated, 'I devote so much of my time to seeing individual and group therapy clients, to supervising and to giving public and professional talks and workshops that I sometimes neglect important theoretical issues for more practical ones' (1989c: 205).

In responding to the critique offered by McBurnett and LaPointe (1978), Ellis (1979a) points out that some of their objections can actually be construed as further support for his biological theory. Here, Ellis debunks their 'task complexity' argument by noting that humans often have difficulty in choosing and carrying out rational choices in a given situation not simply because the task is difficult, but because the task is difficult *for humans*. Thus, in Ellis's (1979a) view, experiencing difficulty with complex tasks constitutes additional evidence for the position that humans have *innate* limitations. He has written that:

> Human difficulties (in making rational decisions or in any other task-solving) obviously are connected with the biologically rooted, species-specific nature of *people*. They never seem to exist in their own right, as McBurnett and LaPointe imply that they do. Precisely because innumerable tasks that humans undertake – from choosing goals and values, to preserving their lives, to enjoying themselves in various ways – present enormous difficulty to them and lead to almost incredibly irrational or self-defeating thinking, emoting, and behaving does it seem reasonably clear that humans are the kind of animal who naturally and easily, and I think through their biological predispositions, behave inefficiently much of the time. (Ellis, 1979a: 114)

REBT and Religion

Criticisms

Ellis (1983f, 1986b) maintains the position that a positive correlation exists between devout religiosity and emotional disturbance. Not surprisingly, this view has been highly unpopular with a good number of theologians and pastoral counsellors. Ellis's views on this issue have been challenged through reference to a number of controlled studies that have failed to support a relationship between religiousness and psychopathology (Bergin, 1983; King, 1978; Sharkey and Maloney, 1986; Stark, 1971; all cited in Johnson, 1992). In addition, some critics have expressed the view that the philosophy underpinning REBT is altogether incompatible with a theistic religious philosophy (with the implication that REBT's use is inappropriate with religious clients).

Ellis (1983f) has suggested that devout religiosity is strongly associated with various manifestations of emotional disturbance, including dependency, intolerance, poor self-esteem and depression. In a recent review of issues pertaining to REBT and religiousness, however, Johnson (1992: 25) makes reference to a number of religious authors who note that religion can have the positive effects of acting as 'a socializing agent, a suppressor of pathology, a perceived source of refuge and a ... form of self therapy via religious expression and activity'. Some writers (for example, McMinn and Lebold, 1989) have expressed the view that Ellis's apparent assumption that devout religious philosophies need to be altered (if individuals are to enjoy good psychological health) is not consistent with a Christian therapeutic approach.

Other aspects of REBT, regarded by religious critics as fundamental to its underlying philosophy, have been identified as features that make it particularly incompatible with theistic religious philosophies. Johnson (1992: 30–1) has written that 'while REP [rational-emotive psychology] advocates atheism, a logical positivist epistemology, situational ethics and responsible hedonism, Judeo-Christian theologies advocate theism, a theistic epistemology, universal (scripture-based) ethics and responsible self-control'. It is here noted that although Johnson (1992) views rational-emotive philosophy as being incompatible with theistic religious philosophies, he is one of a number of writers who nevertheless believe that REBT *can* be used effectively with religious clients.

The veracity of Ellis's religiosity hypothesis has been challenged by a number of studies which failed to find a link between religiousness and emotional disturbance. Johnson briefly reviews this literature in his paper. He concludes that 'empirical research on the relationship between religiousness and mental health suggests no greater incidence of psychopathology among religious persons than among those in the general population' (Johnson, 1992: 26).

Rebuttals

In responding to writers who have criticized his religiosity hypothesis, Ellis (1983f) has attempted to provide clarification of his views. He has pointed out that he no longer believes that religion *per se* creates emotional disturbance; rather, his current view is that *religiosity* (defined by Ellis as devout, dogmatic belief in *any* theological or secular creed) tends to lead to neurosis (Ellis, 1983f, 1992). Thus, Ellis is not critical of *religiousness* or religious commitment unless these terms connote a rigid, absolutistic adherence to a system of beliefs. It appears that some religious critics may fail to recognize that Ellis (1983f, 1992) makes this rather vital distinction.

Ellis has also addressed criticisms that particular aspects of rational-emotive philosophy are incompatible with theistic religious philosophies. He points out, for instance, that REBT does *not* advocate atheism, although Ellis himself is a 'probabilistic' atheist (meaning that he believes the probability that a god exists is extremely low). He has written that 'RET rarely argues against people's holding religious (or other) values but only against their holding these values dogmatically and grandiosely and against their dogmatic claims that such values *must* be observed and followed (by themselves and by others) at all costs' (Ellis, 1992: 38–9). The view that Ellis and other REBT practitioners somehow try to convert religious clients to an atheistic perspective is quite inaccurate.

Ellis also objects to being characterized as a logical positivist. He has indicated that since reading Michael Mahoney's (1976) *Scientist as Subject* he no longer subscribes to this perspective (which accepts as meaningful only those propositions that can be verified by empirical procedures), and that he is now a proponent of critical realism. This position holds that while objects of knowledge exist independently of the knowing mind, knowledge is indirect and proceeds by means of sense data and ideas which are dependent on the mind. Ellis has stated that he presently regards logical positivism as being somewhat dogmatic and unscientific (Ellis, 1992).

Ellis has not explicitly responded to criticisms that REBT's espousal of situational ethics and responsible hedonism make it incompatible with theistic religious philosophies. If, however, one contrasts situational ethics with 'universal (scripture-based) ethics' (as Johnson, 1992, appears to do), it seems reasonable to assume that Ellis would be opposed to the latter if it contains notions of *absolute* standards for human behaviour. If such absolute standards for behaviour *are* considered part and parcel of a theistic religious philosophy, then this may indeed represent a point of irreconcilable difference with rational-emotive philosophy. As regards REBT's value of responsible hedonism, however, the picture may be somewhat different. While Johnson (1992) contrasts responsible hedonism with 'responsible self-control', it may be the case that both of these operating principles will often result in essentially similar choices and behaviours on the parts of the individuals who subscribe to them – unless, of course, 'responsible self-control' carries with it the meaning that all sources of earthly pleasure are to be shunned. Thus, responsible hedonism may be an REBT value that can be taught to and appreciated by religious clients, particularly if it is translated into terms that will help such clients to avoid mistakenly equating it with a heedless pursuit of the pleasures of the flesh.

With respect to the empirical literature reviewed by Johnson (1992) which apparently fails to support his religiosity hypothesis, Ellis (1992) maintains that some of the cited studies can be interpreted as partially confirming his views. Here, he is referring to studies which have utilized the intrinsic/extrinsic scales of the Allport and Ross (1967) Religious Orientation Scale. In describing the differences between intrinsic and extrinsic individuals, Johnson states that 'While the intrinsic person relates religion to all of life and is tolerant and mature, the extrinsic person tends to compartmentalize religion and is prejudiced, immature, and self-serving' (1992: 25). Johnson (1992) cites research indicating that extrinsicness is positively correlated with negatively evaluated psychological characteristics (and uncorrelated with measures of religiousness), while intrinsicness is uncorrelated with negatively evaluated psychological characteristics (and positively correlated with other measures of religiousness). In responding to Johnson's (1992) presentation of this research, Ellis has written that:

> The evidence that Johnson cites in his article partly tends to confirm my view that what Allport and Ross (1967) call extrinsic religion correlates positively with disturbance. But devout believers in anything only partly overlap with what Allport and Ross call extrinsic religionists; and I emphasize their devoutness rather than their 'extrinsicness'. (1992: 38)

With respect to research studying the relationship between religiousness and psychotherapy, Ellis (1992) also cautions that experimenter bias may come into play. Human beings tend to have very strong beliefs concerning the issue of religion, and 'experimenters who hold one view are highly likely to "find" supporting results while those who hold an opposing view are also very likely to "find" confirmatory data' (Ellis, 1992: 39).

Ellis (1992) concurs with Johnson's (1992) view that REBT can be effective with religious clients, particularly when it is somewhat modified in order to accommodate the religious beliefs of such individuals. Other REBT practitioners, such as Young (1989) and DiGiuseppe, Robin and Dryden (1990), have also expressed the view that REBT can be helpful to religious clients without challenging their Judeo-Christian beliefs and values.

REBT, Rationalism and Constructivism

Criticisms

Fairly recently, some cognitive-behavioural theorists have attempted to categorize the various cognitive-behavioural therapies as to whether they fall into 'rationalist' or 'constructivist' camps (Guidano, 1988; Mahoney, 1988). The rationalist position holds that human beings are capable of being accurate perceivers of an objective reality, and emphasizes accurate perception as a means toward optimal functioning in the world. The constructivist position, on the other hand, maintains that humans actively construct their own realities, and that 'objective reality' is unknowable (if, indeed, it exists at all) (Mahoney and Gabriel, 1987; Wessler, 1992). Rather than focusing on whether or not an individual's conception of reality is accurate, constructivist therapies would be concerned with examining whether or not that individual's constructed 'reality' is useful for living in the world. Mahoney (1988) implies that the newly emerging constructivist cognitive-behavioural therapies (Guidano and Liotti, 1983; Joyce-Moniz, 1985) are an improvement over the older rationalist versions, and views REBT (as well as Beck's Cognitive Therapy) as being representative of the latter.

Wessler (1992), in reviewing the rationalist/constructivist dichotomy, takes issue with Mahoney (Mahoney and Gabriel, 1987) insofar as he believes that the current version of REBT *theory* appears constructivistic in its orientation. Here, he is referring to the fact that REBT theory now identifies irrational thinking in terms of beliefs that lead to self-defeating consequences for the individual, rather than primarily defining it in terms of cognitions that represent distortions of 'objective reality'. He states, however, that the actual *practice* of REBT is rationalist in its orientation, as demonstrations and transcripts of Ellis doing therapy suggest that he eschews exploring the personal meanings clients attach to their activating events, and that he attempts to impose seemingly absolutistic criteria for rationality and irrationality on these individuals (for example, the concept that musts and shoulds will of necessity result in emotional disturbance). Wessler's (1992) argument highlights the fact that a concordance does not necessarily exist between a given therapy's theoretical underpinning and its implementation with clients.

Rebuttals

Ellis questions whether the rationalist/constructivist dichotomy really exists with reference to the cognitive-behavioural therapies, and doubts that any of the contemporary versions of this approach can accurately be placed in the rationalist category (Ellis, 1988c). In responding to the view that REBT falls soundly within the rationalist camp, Ellis (1988c, 1990c) has argued that it is actually more constructivistic than the forms of cognitive therapy espoused by some of his constructivist critics (Guidano, 1988; Mahoney, 1988). Some of the specific ways in which REBT can be regarded as constructivistic are as follows:

1 Its theory does not posit absolutistic and invariant criteria for rationality (as some critics wrongly believe); rather, as indicated above, it adopts a more relativistic position and defines rationality in terms of thoughts, feelings and actions that help the individual in the pursuit of personally meaningful goals and purposes.

2 It strongly emphasizes that individuals largely tend to *create* the disturbance-producing beliefs to which they subscribe.

3 Its theory does not take the rationalist position that human reason and intellect represent the sole vehicle to either psychological health or disturbance; instead, it maintains that cognition, emotion and behaviour significantly interact and overlap, and that they cannot accurately be regarded as distinct entities.

In response to Wessler's (1992) argument that while REBT theory is constructivistic, the actual implementation of the therapy is rationalist in nature, Ellis (1993: 531) has stated the following: 'RET has always favored what Beck (1976) calls collaborative empiricism but sometimes, for brevity's sake, it "imposes" irrational or dysfunctional beliefs on clients, then checks to see if the clients really hold them.' Thus, Ellis's concern for efficiency in therapy may be responsible for conveying the impression that he tries to foist absolutistic criteria for rationality and irrationality upon clients. For example, in transcripts and tapes of his therapy sessions it may appear that he is forcefully pushing the concept that subscribing to musts and shoulds *always* results in emotional disturbance. This, however, is not actually his view, as he states in his writings that absolutistic demands will *usually*, but not necessarily, be implicated in clients' emotional problems (Ellis, 1979f, 1989c). Knowing that such demands are quite often involved, he can be reasonably certain that he is therapeutically on target when he actively teaches clients to look for their particular shoulds and musts. By doing this quite early on in therapy, he is frequently able to facilitate efficient treatment.

With reference to the criticism that Ellis does not explore personal meanings with clients, it is noted that he recognizes that human beings are capable of creatively (though self-defeatingly) constructing innumerable musts and shoulds which lead them into disturbances of emotion and behaviour. However, his lengthy tenure as a practising rational emotive behaviour therapist has shown him that a relatively small number of absolutistic demands (with their associated derivatives of awfulizing, I-can't-stand-it-itis and negative person-rating) will typically lead human beings to experience particular types of disturbance. Rather than devoting undue time to 'exploring personal meanings', Ellis is frequently able to anticipate (after getting some basic background information concerning activating events and emotional consequences) the irrational beliefs to which a given client subscribes. Importantly, he will *check with the client* to see if these beliefs are indeed operative before proceeding to show how they may be implicated in the client's upsets.

Seasoned psychotherapists are well aware that no two clients will be exactly alike with respect to the aetiology and presentation of their symptoms; such therapists also recognize that certain similarities and convergences probably exist with respect to the way that human beings become emotionally disturbed. Typically, they employ this knowledge in order to move treatment in directions that they believe will be most helpful to their clients. A truly complete exploration of personal meanings in psychotherapy may represent a fascinating and intellectually challenging exercise, and may indeed prove beneficial for particular clients under certain conditions. In a sense, however, such exploration seems to require that therapists reinvent therapy for each individual with whom they work. This, of course, would not prove very practical, as it would very likely extend treatment time and place a severe strain upon clients' financial resources.

Research Support for REBT's Effectiveness

Criticisms

A number of writers have voiced the concern that REBT's effectiveness has not been adequately assessed through treatment outcome studies. In 1974, Mahoney made the following observation:

> Experimental research evaluating the efficacy of [RET] has been sparse, methodologically poor, and summarily modest in its implications . . . In short, the extent, quality, and findings of the existing experimental work . . . do not warrant an evaluative conclusion. This, of course, means that the clinical efficacy of RET has yet to be adequately demonstrated . . . We are obliged to suspend a more confident judgment until further data are available. (1974: 182)

Despite the fact that twenty years have passed since the publication of Mahoney's (1974) critical commentary, more recent reviewers have voiced similar observations. Haaga and Davison (1989: 195), for example, stated that 'three decades after the initial empirical report on the effectiveness of RET (Ellis, 1957c), even fairly basic questions remain essentially unanswered'. These writers go on to list a number of questions that need to be addressed through sound research:

> (a) Is there any disorder or problem for which RET is a treatment of choice? (b) What proportion of patients achieve clinically significant improvement in RET? (c) What patient and therapist variables predict response to RET, and what predicts relapse after successful RET? (d) Is reduction in irrationality as defined by Ellis a necessary and sufficient condition for change in RET? (Haaga and Davison, 1989: 195)

Dryden (1987b) has also voiced strong concerns about the deficits in the REBT treatment outcome literature. He notes that 'While RET therapists routinely ask their clients: "Where is the evidence . . .?", it is apparent that either they have not asked themselves such questions concerning rational-emotive inspired hypotheses or they have not sought to investigate them' (1987b: 193). In this vein, he notes that between 1983 and 1986, only ten of the articles published in the *Journal of Rational-Emotive and Cognitive-Behavior Therapy* (23.26 per cent of the total number of forty-three published articles) were research articles. Indeed, it does seem clear that a substantial body of quality research on REBT's effectiveness as a psychotherapeutic approach is lacking. It is, in fact, safe to say that the literature detailing (and espousing) the application of REBT to various psychological problems (for example, anxiety, addictions) and modalities (for example, individual, group and family therapy) has outdistanced the accumulated empirical evidence for REBT's efficacy.

Rebuttals

In responding to reviewers who have suggested that the treatment outcome research on REBT is rather sparse and inadequate, Ellis (1989c) concurs that a need exists for additional, carefully designed studies. He notes in particular that while some 200 outcome studies involving REBT have now been done, very few of these studies have actually examined the efficacy of what he refers to as preferential REBT (Ellis, 1989c). As broadly defined by Ellis, preferential REBT 'is almost always comprehensive, multimodal, systematic, and humanistic . . .' (1989c: 230). Most past studies have examined the effectiveness of various forms of cognitive restructuring which fall short of Ellis's criteria for preferential REBT. Thus, despite the fact that many of these studies have supported the effectiveness of cognitive restructuring as a method for helping clients, Ellis (1989c) believes that 'real' REBT has yet to be put to the test. He would like to see a treatment protocol developed for preferential REBT, such

that there would be some degree of standardization (with respect to the treatment that subjects/clients actually receive) between REBT treatment outcome studies (Ellis, personal communication, 1993). To date, no such standard treatment protocol is in existence.

Why is it that REBT treatment outcome research is inadequate in terms of number and quality of studies? Dryden (1987b) has identified several factors that may have contributed to this state of affairs. First, he notes that Ellis is primarily a practitioner and theoretician within the fields of counselling and psychotherapy; thus, his career has not been focused on empirical evaluations of the treatment approach he created. Secondly, Dryden (1987b) notes that REBT (in comparison to other cognitive-behavioural therapies such as Aaron Beck's approach) largely lacks 'centres of excellence' (such as major universities) where the resources for conducting carefully designed treatment outcome studies are more readily available. Thirdly, he observes that major national and international conferences on REBT have tended to be few and far between; as such, a possible vehicle for promoting networking and the exchange of ideas between actual and potential REBT researchers has not been fully exploited. Dryden (1987b) offers the following recommendations for developing an REBT research community and improving the state of REBT treatment research: (a) greater efforts can be made to attract skilled researchers to the parent Institute for REBT in New York City, (b) the *Journal of Rational-Emotive and Cognitive-Behavior Therapy* can encourage submission of a greater number of research papers, and (c) more national and international conferences on REBT can be held.

Conclusions

As the reader is now aware, Ellis and REBT have received critical examination on quite a large number of dimensions. In a sense, the number and variety of these critiques can be regarded as testimony to the complex and provocative nature of Ellis's approach to therapy. Without question, many of his ideas have represented conceptual and philosophical challenges to practitioners and theoreticians holding alternative notions about human change processes.

In turn, these individuals have challenged and stimulated Ellis's thinking with their questions and criticisms. Their critiques have shown him aspects of his ideas that required clarification so that certain needless misunderstandings could be corrected. In addition, these critiques have also at times served as an impetus for Ellis to further develop and refine his theory and therapy. Thanks in part to the efforts of the critics, the REBT of today is more complete and more clearly articulated than the version presented nearly four decades ago.

The process of refinement, however, is probably never truly completed. The criticisms reviewed in this chapter, for example, revealed several issues that Ellis acknowledges may require further attention within REBT:

1 Development of a detailed theory as to how emotions and behaviours may influence thinking processes.
2 Given Ellis's theory on the biological basis of human irrational thinking, formulation of a detailed account of the origin of irrational beliefs in terms compatible with and grounded in the known facts of genetics and neuroscience.
3 Development of an account concerning how environmental influences may contribute to the formation of irrational beliefs.
4 Pursuit of high quality research on the efficacy of preferential REBT, and development of a standard treatment protocol for this approach to be used in research.

Hopefully, in years to come, attempts will be made to address these issues by Ellis or other REBT therapists, theoreticians and researchers.

5

The Overall Influence of Albert Ellis

[N]either Ellis nor the Institute is standing still. Their influence is still expanding in ripples from the rock he dropped into the psychotherapy pool 30 years ago. He seems to have latched on to a fundamental truth of this emerging science: That the human animal's best hope for solving its personal problems is to use its brain as effectively as possible, rationally, according to the dictates of science, without distraction by myths, conventions, or imperatives about behavior.

(Wiener, 1988: 145)

Overview

It is a difficult task to quantify a major figure's overall influence on his or her professional field. In the case of Ellis, however, it is possible to make reference to a number of objective indicants that suggest the degree of impact he has had on the fields of counselling and psychotherapy. As noted in Chapter 1, for instance, a sample of 800 American clinical and counselling psychologists (Smith, 1982) gave Ellis the second-place rating among the ten most influential psychotherapists (he was 'beaten' only by Carl Rogers, who received the first-place rating; Sigmund Freud came third). Also, in an analysis of 14,000 references cited in three major counselling psychology journals published in the United States, Ellis was found to be the most frequently cited author after 1957 (Heesacker, Heppner and Rogers, 1982).

Ellis's influence on the fields of counselling and psychotherapy is also reflected in the number of rational emotive behaviour therapy centres and institutes established in the United States and internationally. Currently, there are ten such organizations in the US, and eight in other countries across the globe. In addition, individuals certified as training faculty members by the Institute for Rational-Emotive Therapy in New York City can be found in Australia, Britain, Canada, Germany, India, Israel, Italy, Mexico, the Netherlands, Turkey and the United States.

The number of professionals who have received Institute-approved training in REBT can be considered as a final objective indicant of Ellis's influence on the mental health field. To date, approximately 3743 therapy practitioners have received the Primary Certificate in REBT after completing a basic training course in rational-emotive theory and techniques; 702 have received the Advanced Certificate, while 656 individuals have completed the more advanced Associate Fellowship and Fellowship training programme at the Institute in New York City (Ellis, personal communication, 1993). Assuming that most of these professionals employ REBT in their work with clients (although they may not necessarily professionally identify themselves as rational emotive behaviour therapists), these numbers attest to the considerable impact that Ellis has had upon contemporary clinical practice.

Having made an attempt to provide the reader with a quantitative appreciation of Ellis's influence on the fields of counselling and psychotherapy, we now shift the focus to a more qualitative review of his major contributions and impact with respect to the mental health field. In particular, we discuss five unique aspects of Ellis's work that make REBT stand out amongst the various psychotherapies. These aspects include Ellis's: (a) strong emphasis on cognition in the creation and treatment of psychological disturbance, (b) philosophical emphasis with respect to promoting enduring change, (c) pioneering work in designing a self-help approach to dealing with psychological problems, (d) emphasis on the importance of an active-directive therapist stance, and (e) views on the nature of the relationship between therapist and client. We then examine factors which may function to limit Ellis's influence within both the lay and professional worlds, and conclude the chapter with a discussion of the future of REBT.

Emphasis on Cognition

Ellis's emphasis on cognition in the creation and treatment of emotional disturbance probably represents one of his most major influences on the fields of counselling and psychotherapy. The recognition that cognition plays an important role in human functioning is not, by any means, a recent development; as noted in Chapter 1, the ancient Greek Stoic philosopher Epictetus observed in the first century AD that 'People are disturbed not by things, but by the views which they take of them.' In addition, certain other writers pre-dated Ellis in giving cognition a place of importance in psychotherapy. For instance, Paul Dubois (1907), in his book *The Psychic Treatment of Nervous Disorders*, espoused the view that 'incorrect ideas' produced psychological distress. With respect to cognition and psychotherapy, Ellis's unique contributions consist of being perhaps the first contemporary mental health practitioner to (a) accord cognition a place of *central* significance in determining either psychological disturbance or health, (b) construct a theory and method of therapy that placed heavy emphasis upon modification of dysfunctional cognitions as the main means to overcome emotional disturbance, and (c) recognize that among the various sorts of cognitions that may be implicated in emotional disturbance, irrational beliefs (that is, evaluative cognitions that are absolutistic in nature) play a central mediating role. Each of these contributions will be discussed separately.

When Ellis first introduced REBT to the therapeutic community in the mid-1950s, he encountered stiff opposition from leading psychoanalytic, client-centred and experiential therapists (Ellis, 1989a). These individuals held differing views as to the origins of human psychological disturbance, and did not believe that Ellis's strong emphasis on helping clients to modify their self-defeating cognitions could lead to any long-lasting or beneficial effects. Proponents of the newly developing field of behaviour therapy also eschewed Ellis's cognitive emphasis, as cognitive processes were not considered to fall into the category of behaviours that were subject to direct observation and measurement. Ellis nevertheless persisted in his efforts to develop and present his ideas to lay and professional audiences, and by the early to mid-1960s a number of other theorists and practitioners were carrying the cognitive-behavioural therapy banner. Some of these early pioneers, such as Aaron T. Beck (1963, 1967), seem to have developed their theories on cognition and disturbance independently of Ellis's influence. Many contributors who arrived on the scene a bit later, however, were very likely influenced by Ellis's ideas (for example, Mahoney, 1974; Spivack and Shure, 1974; Kanfer and Goldstein, 1975; Raimy, 1975; Dyer, 1976; Goldfried and Davison, 1976; Lange and Jakubowski, 1976; Lazarus, 1976; Meichenbaum, 1977; Burns, 1980). Ellis's ABC model – which delineates the relationships between events, cognitions, and emotional and behavioural responses – has been adopted in one form or another by most contemporary schools of cognitive-behavioural therapy.

Prior to Ellis and his initial formulation of REBT, other forms of therapy acknowledged that dysfunctional thinking was implicated in clients' emotional problems. These other approaches, however, usually made comparatively perfunctory attempts to help clients to see and challenge their self-defeating ideas and attitudes. Generally speaking, these therapies emphasized other strategies (for example, catharsis; systematic desensitization) as the main means for giving clients some relief from their emotional distress. Ellis was very likely the first theoretician and practitioner to design a system of therapy that placed primary emphasis on cognitive modification as the major vehicle for effecting helpful changes in affect and behaviour. It should be noted, however, that Ellis recognizes that cognitive modification can be effected through other than cognitive techniques. Thus, in REBT, behavioural and emotive methods are also frequently employed. Ellis, (1982, 1985c) generally refrains from using certain alternative methods, even if some of these might occasionally be helpful to certain clients, as they would tend to shift the focus of therapy away from addressing clients' dysfunctional cognitions. Ellis's strong emphasis upon helping clients to modify dysfunctional cognitions remains unique to the present day, as even most other contemporary cognitive-behavioural approaches to therapy are less discriminating with respect to their choice of intervention techniques.

In his work with clients, Ellis particularly focuses on identifying and disputing irrational beliefs. As the reader will recall, such beliefs are characterized by their absolutistic demanding quality, and are often expressed in the form of musts, shoulds, ought to's and have to's. Amongst contemporary approaches to cognitive-behavioural therapy, Ellis's formulation of REBT is unique for the important role it accords irrational or dysfunctional beliefs in the genesis of emotional disturbance. While other cognitive-behavioural therapies may also attempt to help their clients to challenge shoulds and musts, they fail to emphasize these particular types of cognitions as being central to clients' emotional and behavioural problems. Unlike Ellis and REBT, they are likely to devote a considerable amount of therapy time to identifying and correcting clients' negatively distorted inferences. Ellis acknowledges that distorted inferences may be implicated in clients' emotional problems, but holds the view that such inferences tend to stem from underlying irrational musturbatory beliefs. As such, a focus on modifying these core irrational beliefs will probably result in fewer distorted inferences being generated. It is noted that certain other cognitive-behavioural theorists have started to advance views that are similar to Ellis's in this regard: Aaron T. Beck (Beck, Freeman and associates, 1990), for example, has developed a model wherein clients' underlying 'schemas' are implicated in the production of negatively distorted inferences.

Philosophical Emphasis

Ellis's formulation of REBT makes it unique among modern psychotherapies insofar as it contains an explicit and well-articulated philosophical emphasis. REBT's philosophical emphasis is expressed in two main ways.

First, Ellis and REBT have been quite specific in outlining criteria for psychological health (see Chapter 2). These criteria represent a much clearer articulation of therapeutic 'values' than that found in almost any other therapeutic system. REBT promotes these values (such as long-range hedonism, flexibility, self-acceptance and scientific thinking) because it holds that if individuals work at adopting them they will have a much greater chance at minimizing emotional misery and maximizing survival and happiness. These values are regarded as 'good' because of their survival-and happiness-enhancing potential, and can be viewed as constituting the tenets of a rational philosophy of living. No other secular approach to therapy has been as explicit in outlining a specific philosophy for living.

Second, Ellis has long emphasized that the most helpful and enduring therapeutic changes occur on a philosophical level. This emphasis deviates from the approach taken by most other psycho-therapies, including alternative forms of cognitive-behavioural treatment. To cite an example, consider the case of a young female client who fears (and avoids) socializing because she is convinced that if she makes social overtures to other people, she will certainly be rejected. Many cognitive-behavioural therapists would attempt to help this client to overcome her social anxiety by designing homework assignments wherein she attends social functions and makes friendly overtures to some of the other people in attendance. Hopefully, after enacting a series of such homework assignments, the client would accumulate evidence that rejection experiences are far less common than she had believed. Thus, she may experience symptomatic relief (in terms of becoming less anxious and avoidant) because she has achieved change at the inferential level – she no longer makes predictions that she will always be rejected. Rational emotive behaviour therapists would also try to help the client to change at the philosophical level. If the client does not accomplish change at the philosophical level – in terms of not *awfulizing* about rejection experiences and rating herself as a *complete loser* should they occur – then there is a likelihood that she will revert back to her earlier levels of anxiety and avoidance if confronted by a number of negative activating events (for example, a string of apparent rejections). Rather than focusing primarily on changing clients' negatively distorted inferences, Ellis (and other REBT practitioners) will initially accept these inferences as if they were true and then work to help clients to identify, dispute and challenge their irrational beliefs. Here, the goal is to assist clients in internalizing an anti-awfulizing, non-person-rating, anti-I-can't-stand-it-itis philosophy that will help them to avoid upsets across a variety of situations and contexts. It is inevitable that individuals will encounter numerous negative activating events as they proceed through life; by working at the philosophical level Ellis hopes to help his clients to overcome their present-day emotional problems and to become less vulnerable to emotional disturbance in the future.

Self-help Approach

Ellis and REBT have always placed an emphasis upon the importance of client effort in the process of overcoming emotional and behavioural dysfunctions. In Ellis's view, clients who apply his dictum of 'work and practice' are more likely to effect beneficial, long-lasting changes in their self-defeating personal philosophies. Clients who work with Ellis (and other REBT therapists) in therapy are usually quickly disabused of the notion that their therapist will magically do something to them during their therapy sessions that will somehow 'cure' them of their problems. Clients are taught concepts, skills and techniques that they can utilize to combat their irrational beliefs and are encouraged to apply these things outside of sessions to make therapeutic gains without the presence of a supervising therapist.

Within his therapy practice, Ellis emphasizes a self-help approach to clients in a number of different ways. He does this by promoting and encouraging client use of homework assignments, self-help work sheets and psychoeducational materials.

Ellis did not invent the concept of therapeutic homework assignments for clients, but he was one of the very first psycho-therapists to employ such assignments in a relatively systematic, consistent manner within a general psychotherapy practice (other early pioneers of homework assignments in therapy include Andrew Salter, 1949; George Kelly, 1955; Joseph Wolpe, 1958). He prompts his clients to work independently at challenging their irrational beliefs during nearly every one of his therapy sessions, and very often encourages them to undertake action assignments (such as shame-attacking and risk-taking exercises) that will help them to accomplish this in a particularly forceful way. He conducts follow-up to determine whether clients have actually enacted their homework assignments between sessions, and will spend session time helping them to identify and overcome any cognitive obstacles (such as the irrational belief, 'It's *too damn hard* to work at my therapy between sessions!') to homework implementation. Clients who consistently complete therapeutically meaningful homework assignments will probably benefit more quickly from treatment, and may also be more likely to attribute positive changes to their own (as opposed to their therapist's) efforts. Such attributions can be quite helpful, as they may strengthen clients' beliefs in their personal efficacy and their ability to function independently.

As mentioned in Chapter 3, Ellis has designed a homework self-help form which is intended for client use on an independent basis (Sichel and Ellis, 1984). It helps clients to structure their attempts at disputing their irrational beliefs by providing spaces for filling in the A's, B's and C's of an emotional upset, and lists common irrational beliefs to facilitate the task of identifying unhelpful cognitions. Ellis often recommends to his clients that they use these homework sheets between sessions, and will sometimes review them during sessions.

Ellis has also pioneered a self-help approach to therapy through the numerous rational-emotive texts he has authored for lay people. He has, in fact, written a greater number of self-help books than any other major psychotherapy theorist. These books tend to be quite practical in nature, as they provide clear explications of the origins of various types of disturbance as well as guidelines for overcoming these problems. The most popular of Ellis's self-help books (in terms of total volumes sold over time) is a *New Guide to Rational Living* (Ellis and Harper, 1975) which deals with problem areas such as anxiety, depression, lack of self-discipline, fear of failure and the dire need for approval. To date, this book has sold approximately 1.5 million copies, and has been translated into several languages. The following is a very partial list of other REBT self-help books authored (or co-authored) by Ellis across his career as a psychotherapist:

A Guide to Successful Marriage (with Robert Harper, 1961)

How to Live with a Neurotic (1975)

Anger: How to Live With and Without It (1977g)

Overcoming Procrastination (with William Knaus, 1977)

A Guide to Personal Happiness (with Irving Becker, 1982)

How to Stubbornly Refuse to Make Yourself Miserable about Anything – Yes, Anything! (1988b)

Why Am I Always Broke? How to Be Sane About Money (with Patricia Hunter, 1991)

The Art and Science of Rational Eating (with Michael Abrams and Lidia Dengelegi, 1992)

When AA Doesn't Work for You: Rational Steps to Quitting Alcohol (with Emmett Velten, 1992)

In addition to his many books for laypersons, Ellis has also produced (primarily through the Institute for Rational-Emotive Therapy) numerous audiotapes that provide self-help guidelines for dealing with problems such as low frustration tolerance, shame, addictions, procrastination, non-assertiveness and anger.

A fairly large number of rational-emotive self-help books have been published by authors other than Ellis. As a result, it is probably safe to say that REBT has had a greater impact on the audience of lay readers interested in self-help approaches to therapy than any other legitimate system of counselling or psychotherapy in existence.

Conceivably, lay persons who utilize REBT self-help books, audiotapes and homework aids in a determined and consistent fashion could experience considerable success in overcoming their emotional and behavioural problems without ever consulting a therapist. The self-help approach to therapy has its limitations, however, and a good number of individuals (because of low frustration tolerance, the severity of their disturbance or other factors) have difficulty keeping themselves focused on the hard work of making themselves less disturbed. Such individuals may benefit most from using self-help materials in combination with consultations with an appropriately trained therapist.

Active-directive Approach

In his book, *Reason and Emotion in Psychotherapy*, Ellis begins his discussion on active-directive therapy by noting that:

> Most of the major and most highly publicized schools of psychotherapy, especially the classical Freudian school at one end of the scale and the Rogerian non-directive or client-centred school at the other end of the scale, roundly abjure active-directive modes of therapy and enthusiastically favour passive-indirect modes.
>
> Devotees of these non-directive methods hold that patients must be very close to achieving significant insights for themselves before the therapist's interpretation can be effective; that a therapist's authoritarian presentation encourages continued dependency on the patient's part; that directive techniques are highly undemocratic and ethically unjustified;

that the patient has enormous potentials for growth within himself and that this potential can be best released if the therapist is non-directive; and that other serious disadvantages ensue when the therapist is highly active or interpretive. (1962: 189)

Disciples of passive-indirect modes of therapy also tend to believe that too much direction and activity on the therapist's part will jeopardize rapport with clients, and that a so-called 'frontal assault' on clients' 'defences' can lead to premature termination or even a psychotic episode.

Despite the fact that therapist passivity and non-directiveness were advocated by the most popular therapeutic approaches of the 1950s, Ellis began experimenting with an increasingly active-directive style in his own clinical practice. He did so partly because of his dissatisfaction with the results he was obtaining with his clients through psychoanalysis and psychoanalytically oriented psychotherapy.

In his pioneering work as an active-directive therapist, Ellis (1962) observed that the negative effects predicted by passive-indirect therapists failed to occur in his own practice with any great frequency. Instead, he found that most of his clients benefited when he actively taught them the principles and techniques of rational emotive behaviour therapy. He discovered that it was usually unnecessary to wait for clients to be 'ready' to attain important insights, as logic and reason could quite often be employed to demonstrate the validity of particular rational-emotive interpretations (Ellis, 1977h). Ellis also found that any upsets clients experienced in relation to his relatively confrontational stance could be effectively dealt with by uncovering and challenging the irrational beliefs behind the upset. Thus, if a given male client felt guilty after being confronted with evidence of his passive-aggressive behaviour toward his wife, Ellis would quickly show him how he was needlessly and inappropriately damning himself for being a fallible human being.

Ellis (1962) also found that an active-directive therapist stance, in combination with a no-nonsense, problem-focused approach, helped to make his clients less, rather than more, dependent upon him. As his clients proceeded through REBT and acquired the tools for overcoming their disturbance, they gained confidence in their ability to function as their own therapists. Ellis (1979f) has always advocated helping clients to become more independent, rational thinkers.

Ellis (1976a, 1987a) concurs with the position that human beings have enormous potential for growth, but he also maintains that they are quite talented at creating and tenaciously adhering to self-defeating irrational beliefs. Given this perspective, he takes issue with the view that non-directive therapies provide the optimal environment for helping individuals to realize their growth potential. Clients very often come to therapy and counselling because they are in considerable confusion over how best to reduce their emotional misery and actualize themselves, and a therapist who passively refuses to offer guidance in this regard may quite frequently be viewed as unhelpful and ineffective. Ellis has noted that:

> The patient comes to therapy asking for help; the therapist, because of his own prejudices, maintains a passive attitude and refuses to give any substantial help; so the patient, quite naturally I believe, 'resists' the therapist and often ends up by quitting the relationship. (1962: 194)

Ellis believes that when the therapist actively instructs the client on the means to ameliorate disturbance and approach self-actualization, better therapeutic outcomes are generally attained.

With respect to concerns that too much therapist activity and directiveness will damage rapport with clients, Walen, DiGiuseppe and Dryden noted the following:

> Rapport . . . *can* be developed when the therapist behaves directively . . . This point was particularly evident to us while co-leading therapy groups with Dr Ellis. As directive as he is, the group members frequently reported feelings of warmth and respect for 'Al.' When questioned by us, group members reported that he demonstrated his concern by his many questions, his complete attention to their problems, and his advocacy of an accepting and tolerant philosophy, and by teaching them something immediate that they could do to reduce their pain. (1992: 44)

Thus, it appears that an active-directive approach, when implemented properly, can actually facilitate the development of rapport with clients. And, of course, good rapport within the therapeutic relationship tends to mitigate the possibility of premature termination by therapy clients. With respect to this issue, Ellis has observed that:

> this procedure of actively assailing the patient's resistance has its own dangers, especially that of his leaving therapy. I find in actual practice, however, that few of my patients do leave for this reason and that still fewer experience the pernicious effects, such as psychotic breaks, which the professional literature so cavalierly assumes that they will experience if their defences are directly assaulted. (1962: 195)

Ellis was not the first therapist to utilize an active-directive approach to therapy – Adler (1927, 1929), for example, pre-dated Ellis in favouring direct intervention by therapists. Ellis did become one of the main champions and promoters of this approach, however, at a time when it was not widely accepted within the therapeutic community. Active-directive therapy is now widely accepted and practised. It is part and parcel of the current approaches to behavioural and cognitive-behavioural treatment, and has even been melded with psychoanalytic methods to produce brief forms of psychodynamic therapy. It is likely that Ellis's strong efforts contributed to the widespread acceptance of active-directive therapy and the respect in which it is now held.

Nature of the Therapeutic Relationship

Just as Ellis advocates that therapists adopt an active-directive stance with their clients, he also recommends that they refrain from providing these individuals with an excessive amount of 'oozing warmth' and love (Ellis, 1991c). In his view, clients will usually derive greater benefits from a hard-headed, no-nonsense approach to solving their psychological problems. In maintaining this position at an early point in his career as a psychotherapist, Ellis again deviated from the views espoused by some of the more 'established' therapies of the 1950s and 1960s.

It should be noted that Ellis's cautionary views on excessive therapist warmth and love within the therapeutic relationship were at least partly the outcome of his own early experimentation with alternative approaches to treatment. As described in Chapter 3, in the early 1950s he tried Ferenczi's (1952) method of providing his clients with considerable warmth and support (Ellis, 1991c). While many clients seemed to love this approach (and, indeed, wanted to schedule more sessions per week and probably stayed in therapy for a longer period of time), Ellis found that a good number of them seemed to get worse instead of better. In particular he noted that they tended to become more (instead of less) dependent upon him, and that they self-defeatingly increased their low frustration tolerance and needs for love and approval. He subsequently abandoned Ferenczi's approach and began to experiment with the methods and techniques that he would eventually synthesize as REBT.

Ellis is concerned with helping his clients to make therapeutic gains as efficiently as possible. With this goal in mind, his approach to therapy involves quickly zeroing in on clients' self-defeating irrational beliefs and showing them how to challenge and replace these with more self-helping rational beliefs. Thus, Ellis's REBT sessions tend to be very focused upon psychological problem-solving, with relatively little time being devoted to small talk and social relating between client and therapist. This, however, does not mean that Ellis promotes therapist aloofness and disinterest within the therapeutic relationship. On the contrary, he advocates a number of therapeutic methods and strategies that can tend to facilitate rapport with clients and make REBT sessions quite emotionally evocative for them.

With respect to the issue of rapport-building with clients, it is noted that Ellis's problem-focused approach quite often communicates to clients that he is vitally interested in helping them to overcome their emotional misery and to lead happier lives. It is probably safe to say that many human beings will tend to develop positive feelings toward a therapist who appears so intent upon offering them meaningful assistance.

Ellis's rapport with and impact on clients is probably further enhanced by his uses of unconditional acceptance, self-disclosure and humour. In offering unconditional acceptance to his clients, Ellis refrains from judging them negatively in their totality, even when they act in particularly unethical or obnoxious ways. He thus tries to present himself as a tolerant and 'forgiving' therapist, in the hope that clients will become better able to tolerate and forgive themselves when they behave in a less than exemplary fashion. Ellis does not hesitate to engage in self-disclosure with his clients during his therapy sessions, which he typically uses to show how he overcame some of his own emotional and behavioural problems earlier in life. This sort of self-disclosure can teach clients the means for dealing with various sorts of psychological problems, show them that they need not feel ashamed about having psychological problems themselves, and help them to view their therapist as a fellow human being. Ellis's use of humour also promotes a degree of familiarity and ease within his relationships with clients, while at the same time demonstrating to them the absurd and exaggerated nature of the irrational beliefs to which they subscribe. In addition to serving as vehicles for enhancing rapport, Ellis's use of unconditional acceptance, self-disclosure, and humour also help his therapy sessions to be more vivid and memorable for clients.

Despite Ellis's oft-stated cautions about therapists offering their clients an overabundance of warmth within the therapeutic relationship, a good number of therapists still view therapist warmth as an almost essential component of helpful treatment. For many other mental health practitioners, however, Ellis has effectively demonstrated that such warmth is hardly a necessity, and that it may in fact impede therapy and have deleterious consequences for clients. Ellis's therapeutic work has provided some measure of evidence that many clients can 'survive' and substantially benefit from a therapeutic relationship in which a strong problem-solving focus is a key element.

Limitations to Ellis's Influence

In an overall sense, Ellis and REBT have had a profound impact upon the fields of counselling and psychotherapy. It appears, however, that Ellis's impact has been somewhat limited within certain constituencies. He and his ideas are, for instance, not well understood or well-regarded by a still substantial segment of the mental health community. Further, it is noted that his name and his therapy are simply unknown to a great number of laypersons. Unlike Freud and psychoanalysis, Ellis and REBT have yet to become household words.

What are the various factors that may operate to limit Ellis's (and REBT's) influence? Several potential ones can be identified. First, we will discuss factors that may function to limit Ellis's influence among laypersons. We will then turn attention to discussion of factors that may limit the impact that he and his ideas have had upon mental health professionals.

Factors Limiting Ellis's Impact upon Laypersons

While it is safe to say that by this point many thousands of laypersons have probably had some form of exposure (either through actual therapy, workshops, publications, lectures, or radio and television broadcasts) to Ellis's views concerning psychotherapy and emotional disturbance, it is also accurate to observe that most people don't go about spouting terms such as 'irrational beliefs' and 'awfulizing' in the same way that they might make reference to such things as 'the unconscious' and 'the superego'. Ellis's name and ideas have not yet made inroads into the lay lexicon in the manner accomplished by Freud and his ideas. Perhaps this phenomenon will occur with time, but it can be noted that there may be a number of reasons why Ellis and REBT aren't better known and accepted among the population-at-large.

Ellis's manner of presenting his ideas to the public may represent one factor which limits his impact and appeal for many individuals. With his occasionally flamboyant and sometimes irreverent public speaking style, he may violate the expectations of a good number of people as to what a respectable psychotherapist 'should' be like. Persons attending one of his many public workshops or lectures may believe at the outset that they are going to be exposed to a speaker who fits the stereotyped image of an established psychologist: an intellectually lofty individual who maintains an appropriate degree of professional decorum while still conveying considerable warmth. Thus, they may be somewhat shocked to discover that Ellis often sprinkles a good measure of profanity throughout his public presentations, and that he voices strong views on a number of topics that may be close to their hearts. It is likely that a fairly large segment of the public finds his view on the connection between religiosity and emotional disturbance to be offensive. Many other individuals may be offended by his position on self-responsibility for emotional disturbance, as they are psychologically invested in believing that their current life circumstances or poor upbringing are responsible for their present-day emotional problems. When a speaker is seen as attacking his audience's cherished beliefs, the probability that his message will be rejected is likely to increase.

Portions of Ellis's public audience may also be non-receptive to his views on psychotherapy and emotional disturbance because they appear (at first glance) to be too simplistic to be of much meaningful use for improving the quality of one's life. Having had some degree of previous exposure to Freudian arcana, they hold the belief that proposed solutions to emotional problems must be complex, confusing and quite mysterious in order to be effective. This was, in fact, the view held by the first author of this volume while still a beginning graduate student in clinical psychology. After hearing his first audiotaped Ellis lecture, I (J.Y.) remarked to a fellow student that I was unable to see much therapeutic utility in 'helping clients to change how they talk to themselves'. Surely, the process of 'curing' emotional disturbance must be more complicated than that!

In addition to appearing too simplistic, REBT may simply not be 'sexy' enough to capture the public's imagination. Certainly, deeply repressed sexual and aggressive impulses (*à la* Freud) are going to be more fascinating to the well-read layperson as a cause for emotional disturbance than are fairly easily accessible shoulds and musts. Also, Ellis strongly emphasizes the value of determined 'work and practice' with respect to challenging and overcoming the irrational beliefs that underpin psychological problems. Unfortunately, 'work and practice' require time and effort, and many people would prefer to believe that there are fairly easy and painless solutions to their emotional ills. Being reluctant to recognize that the best way to solve their problems is to fully face them, they tend to gravitate toward therapeutic approaches that absolve them from personal responsibility and require little more than regular attendance of therapy sessions.

Factors Limiting Ellis's Influence among Professionals
Ellis's influence among mental health professionals has probably been limited by some of the same factors which have limited his influence with the lay public. Thus, some therapy practitioners may be turned off by Ellis and his ideas because they find his views too strong and his theory too simplistic. Other mental health professionals – particularly those with strong research backgrounds – may discount Ellis's theory and therapy because they see inadequacies in the research literature which supports REBT's clinical efficacy.

Ellis (1982, 1983a; Ellis and Yeager, 1989) has strongly voiced his views concerning the limitations and potential dangers of numerous alternative approaches to therapy. These views are perhaps not too likely to arouse the ire of fellow mental health practitioners when they are directed at non-mainstream approaches such as Reichian or transpersonal therapies. When, however, Ellis criticizes popularly practised therapies (such as client-centred therapy and psychoanalytic approaches to treatment) as being largely ineffective, inefficient or potentially harmful, he is more likely to offend significant segments of the therapeutic community. His criticisms – often expressed quite vigorously in his writings, lectures and REBT demonstrations – may well arouse resistance to his ideas among both therapists and clients who have been involved with therapies other than REBT. Clients who have attended psychoanalytic sessions for a number of years, for instance, may not be too receptive to hearing that some of the 'insights' they have attained (such as the manner in which their upbringing has determined their present-day problems in living) are just so much 'Freudian horseshit'. Similarly, therapists who have been invested for years in the practice of one of the therapeutic approaches which Ellis criticizes will often be non-receptive to hearing their professional work dismissed as unhelpful and in some cases actually harmful to clients. Many psychotherapists derive a sense of their professional identity from the type of therapy that they practise; this professional identity, in turn, can become one of the major bases upon which they (irrationally) define their personhood. As a perceived assault upon one's professional identity may then be experienced as an attack upon one's personhood, it is not at all surprising that a great number of non-REBT therapists (defensively) reject Ellis's opinions on what constitutes effective and helpful treatment.

A good number of psychotherapy practitioners may be non-receptive to the theory and therapy which Ellis has constructed because they view REBT as being too simplistic. Psychoanalytically trained therapists in particular may be prone to be critical of REBT because in their view it deals only with the conscious or preconscious thinking of the individual. From their perspective, the treatment effects of Ellis's therapy will of necessity be very limited since REBT practice basically ignores the existence of 'the unconscious'. This criticism is made despite the fact that psychoanalytic therapists themselves work with clients' conscious or preconscious cognitions, and usually define unconscious material as being largely inaccessible in a direct sense.

Other therapists from behavioural and cognitive-behavioural backgrounds may view REBT as oversimplifying the complex inter-relationships between cognitions, emotions and behaviours, and may hold it in low regard for placing such a strong emphasis upon identifying and challenging clients' irrational beliefs. While Ellis and REBT do indeed emphasize the role played by irrational beliefs in producing emotional disturbance, it is simply inaccurate to claim that they do not acknowledge the many ways in which thoughts, feelings and behaviours can interact and importantly affect each other. Ellis places a particular focus upon modifying irrational beliefs, but he also advocates that therapists employ a variety of cognitive, emotive and behavioural techniques in order to most effectively help clients to overcome their psychological problems.

It is also possible that some mental health professionals are turned off by REBT because of some of the coined terminology that Ellis has employed to describe key aspects of REBT's theory. Thus, the term 'musturbation' is used to describe the process of subscribing to an irrational belief, while the phrase 'I-can't-stand-it-itis' is used to describe the outcome of holding irrational demands for comfort and safety. Ellis has used these invented terms as a means for increasing his impact upon his audience at lectures and workshops; unfortunately, they can also make REBT seem somewhat contrived and non-scholarly. For therapists accustomed to having theoretical concepts expressed in more intellectual terms, Ellis's homespun jargon may incorrectly be interpreted as evidence that there is little of substance in his theories.

As noted earlier, some academic psychologists may have some reservations about REBT as a therapeutic approach because of inadequacies in the research literature which purports to back its clinical efficacy. In particular, as noted in Chapter 4, this literature has been criticized for (a) failing to identify particular problems for which REBT is the treatment of choice, (b) failing to indicate what proportion of patients achieve clinically significant improvement in REBT, (c) neglecting to identify patient and therapist variables which predict response to REBT, (d) neglecting to identify factors that may be predictive of relapse after successful REBT and (e) failing to provide strong evidence in support of the notion that reduction in irrational thinking is a major condition for therapeutic change in REBT (Haaga and Davison, 1989). Ellis (1989c) himself has offered the observations that preferential REBT has yet to be put to the test in carefully designed treatment outcome studies, and that there is a need to develop a standard treatment protocol for preferential REBT in order to help ensure that meaningful comparisons can be made within and between treatment outcome studies. There certainly is room for growth and refinement within the REBT treatment outcome literature, and this issue has received attention from some major rational emotive behaviour and cognitive-behavioural therapists (see, for example, Dryden, 1987b; Kendall, Haaga, Ellis, Bernard, DiGiuseppe and Kassinove, manuscript submitted for publication). Hopefully, in the not too distant future, studies will be implemented which help to address some of the research weaknesses identified by REBT's critics. It is, however, important to note that for any particular type of psychotherapy, even the most impressive body of research support would not guarantee universal acceptance of that specific approach to treatment. Psychotherapists can tend to become overly enamoured of their particular therapeutic orientations, so that they are able to selectively dismiss any data that fail to confirm their biases as to what constitutes effective treatment. If therapists were actually to choose their approaches to treatment on the basis of the accumulated empirical literature on psychotherapy, it would probably be the case that a number of still-popular approaches would virtually be extinct.

The Future of REBT

Since the mid-1950s, when Ellis first introduced 'rational therapy' to the psychotherapeutic community, REBT has attracted the attention of a large number of mental health practitioners. Many of these individuals have themselves become enthusiastic proponents of this approach to therapy, and have made their own important contributions to its theory and practice. Given the fact that REBT continues to attract the interest and efforts of new generations of mental health professionals, it seems likely that it will continue to benefit from new developments and refinements as it enters its fourth decade of existence. In this section we speculatively examine the future of REBT in five different spheres: technique refinement, psychoeducational applications, the managed mental health care environment, expansion of areas of application and research.

Refinement of Techniques

Ellis has indicated that he uses his experiences as a practising clinician to work at refining REBT (Yankura and Dryden, 1990). As he and other REBT practitioners have a high degree of interest in continuing to develop REBT as an efficient and effective approach to treatment, it is quite possible that the future will see continuing advances in the efficacy of rational-emotive treatment strategies and techniques.

Ellis has identified one particular area in which he sees technique refinement as being particularly important. He notes that while REBT can be very effective at helping clients to deal with their self-worth issues and to overcome their ego disturbance, it has a more difficult time helping them to overcome their discomfort disturbance (Bernard, 1986; Ellis, 1987a, 1987c). This is an interesting observation, considering the fact that REBT was the first psychotherapeutic system to explicitly recognize and emphasize the manner in which clients' absolutistic demands for comfort can contribute to significant problems in living. Clients who strongly subscribe to such demands (which result in discomfort disturbance) will self-defeatingly procrastinate on important tasks, go for short-range pleasures at the expense of long-range goals, and 'resist' enacting homework assignments that involve exposure to uncomfortable situations. While Ellis has found certain strategies to be useful in helping clients to overcome some of the self-defeating behaviours stemming from their discomfort disturbance (such as teaching clients how to use rewards and penalties with themselves so that they are more likely to undertake avoided tasks), he is aware that these strategies have serious limitations (for example, some clients will self-defeatingly neglect to apply penalties to themselves when appropriate). Ellis (interviewed in Bernard, 1986) has speculated that it may be possible to create high-impact educational devices (such as films and cartoons) that will effectively teach children and adults the advantages of long-range hedonism and the disadvantages of being over-focused on obtaining immediate gratification. Perhaps exposing individuals to such high impact educational devices at an early age will help to mitigate the likelihood of their developing significant problems with discomfort disturbance later in life. Development of these sorts of materials, as well as a general focus on designing better ways for helping clients in therapy to overcome this particular problem, will be a fruitful area for continued efforts by REBT practitioners.

Psychoeducational Developments

As indicated in the preceding section, Ellis believes that rational-emotive educational materials can be developed which will help clients to overcome (or avoid developing) emotional and behavioural problems. In fact, he has long advocated expanding the psychoeducational aspects of REBT in order that it might be routinely taught to laypeople in a variety of contexts (Ellis and Grieger, 1977; Dames and Ellis, 1991). The business world and the educational system represent two particular arenas in which such expansion might be pursued.

A number of attempts have already been made to design and implement rational-emotive psychoeducational programmes in schools, and a variety of teaching materials are available for doing so. These materials include publications such as William Knaus's (1974) *Rational-Emotive Education: A Manual for Elementary School Teachers*, and Ann Vernon's (1989a, b) two-volume set (for grades 1–12) entitled *Thinking, Feeling, Behaving: An Emotional Education Curriculum for Children*. Rational-emotive principles have also been attractively packaged in the Pumsy programme (marketed by Timberline Press) for helping children to deal with self-worth issues (Pumsy is the name of a dragon character designed as a vehicle for maintaining children's interest in the programme). With respect to efforts to include emotional education within schools' general educational curricula, it is noted that a current trend in education within the United States is toward maintaining emotionally disturbed children (as well as children with other sorts of educational disabilities) within regular mainstream classrooms (as opposed to segregating them within separate special education classrooms). If the inclusion movement persists as an educational trend, it could ultimately result in increased systematic efforts to find ways of teaching children in school how to deal with their emotional upsets and the negative activating events they experience in their lives. With its comparatively early start in this area, REBT could conceivably be at the forefront in advising educational administrators how to design, implement and evaluate emotional education programmes within school systems.

With respect to the business arena, the Institute for Rational-Emotive Therapy markets a variety of psychoeducational products for use in business contexts. These include the publication *Rational Effectiveness Training: Increasing Personal Productivity at Work* (DiMattia and Mennen, 1990) and the audiotape series *Mind over Myths: Managing Difficult Situations in the Workplace* (Rational Effectiveness Training Systems, 1987). DiMattia (1993) has noted that the Institute has trained hundreds of employee assistance programme (EAP) professionals in the use of REBT as an assessment and referral tool; he makes the observation that REBT can have applicability to many of the priorities of the business world, including increasing productivity, conducting effective performance appraisals, developing communication skills, increasing sales effectiveness, stress management and conflict resolution. It is very likely that in years to come, the applications of REBT within the corporate sphere will increase and expand.

REBT and the Managed Health Care Environment

Within the United States, managed health care corporations are playing an increasing role in the administration of health insurance benefits. These corporations seek to contain health care costs, partly by reviewing whether particular treatments and procedures are medically warranted. Within the mental health field, managed health care corporations are requiring increased accountability from therapy practitioners. This means, in part, that practitioners must provide clearly articulated therapeutic goals and provide treatment that is deemed (by the managed care corporation) to be both effective and of reasonable duration.

REBT therapists (along with practitioners of other types of cognitive-behavioural therapy and behaviour therapy) are in a good position to satisfy these accountability requirements. This is due largely to the fact that they are accustomed to conceptualizing cognitive, emotional and behavioural goals for treatment in comparatively clear-cut terms, and also to their interest in conducting therapy as efficiently as possible. Winegar (1992) has noted that clinicians as a group will need increased familiarity with short-term therapies, as these therapies are philosophically compatible with managed care values and insurance benefit constraints. Thus, if present trends continue, REBT may become even more widely practised (at least in the United States) than it already is. On the other hand, therapeutic approaches that require multiple sessions per week for many years (such as classical Freudian psychoanalysis) may rapidly experience a thinning of the ranks with respect to the number of practitioners willing to use them.

Expansion of Areas of Application

REBT has long been regarded by its advocates as having applicability to a large variety of clinical disorders and various sorts of problems in living. Nevertheless, most of the available REBT practitioners' guidebooks available up until the early 1980s were general presentations on how to implement this approach to therapy. Fairly recently, however, a number of books have been added to the REBT literature which provide more detailed descriptions on applying REBT to specific clinical problem areas. These publications include *Anxiety Disorders: A Rational-Emotive Approach* (Warren and Zgourides, 1991), *Rational-Emotive Therapy with Alcoholics and Substance Abusers* (Ellis, McInerney, DiGiuseppe and Yeager, 1988), and *Rational-Emotive Therapy with Children and Adolescents* (Bernard and Joyce, 1984). This apparent trend towards increased specificity in describing REBT's application to various disorders and problems may reflect a particular developmental stage of maturation for REBT as a clinical approach. An accumulated body of clinical lore (stemming from practitioner experience and relevant research findings on REBT and cognitive-behavioural therapy) has now made it possible to describe some of the nuances and complexities involved in treating clinical problems such as anxiety disorders and addictions. It is possible that this trend will continue and new practitioners' manuals will appear describing the specifics of applying REBT to additional clinical disorders.

The advent of Rational Recovery (RR) represents a significant expansion of REBT's application in the area of addictions recovery. Rational Recovery is a network of addictions recovery self-help groups (developed by Jack Trimpey, CSW) that utilizes rational-emotive principles and techniques to help recovering alcoholics and substance abusers manage the emotional and behavioural difficulties typically inherent in the recovery process. Rational Recovery represents a viable alternative for individuals interested in participating in a self-help group without the religious overtones of twelve-step programmes such as Alcoholics Anonymous (AA) and Narcotics Anonymous (NA). Meetings of Rational Recovery groups are conducted by laypersons (as are AA and NA meetings); however, each RR group has a trained rational emotive behaviour therapist available for consultation on an as-needed *pro bono* basis. The principles of Rational Recovery are described in the publication entitled *Rational Recovery from Alcoholism: The Small Book* (Trimpey, 1992). Though still at a fairly early stage of development, Rational Recovery groups appear to be growing in number and popularity across the United States.

Future Directions for Research on REBT
Recent roundtable discussions by a number of prominent rational emotive behaviour and cognitive-behavioural therapists yielded an important steering paper entitled 'Rational-Emotive Therapy in the 1990s and Beyond: Current Status, Recent Revisions, and Research Questions' (Kendall, Haaga, Ellis, Bernard, DiGiuseppe and Kassinove, manuscript submitted for publication). Kendall et al.

state their observation that while REBT has had a profound impact on the professional *practice* of psychotherapy, as a *theory* of psychopathology it does not enjoy as strong a scientific reputation. With their paper, Kendall et al. hope to redress this situation by providing guidance and motivation for future research endeavours. They describe research priorities in three vital areas: (a) assessment, (b) REBT's theory of psychopathology and (c) the practice of REBT.

With respect to assessment in REBT, Kendall et al. highlight the need for research which would be focused on refining techniques for measuring irrational beliefs. Such refinements would improve treatment outcome research on REBT by making it possible to examine more clearly the relationship between therapeutic gains and decrements in clients' irrational thinking. Also with respect to treatment outcome studies, Kendall et al. emphasize the importance of developing procedures for measuring the integrity and competence with which therapists employ rational-emotive principles and techniques. Within comparative research studies, these procedures would be particularly important in distinguishing the effects of REBT from those of alternative therapeutic approaches (especially with respect to other, partially overlapping cognitive-behavioural treatments).

With regard to REBT's theory of psychopathology, Kendall et al. describe the following research priorities:

1 Re-establish (with improved measures of irrational beliefs) the correlation between irrational beliefs and emotional distress.
2 Investigate *disorder-specific* rational-emotive hypotheses (that is, examine whether specific types of irrational beliefs are associated with discrete disorders, such as panic disorder).
3 Investigate whether irrational beliefs are better conceptualized as states or traits.
4 Test Ellis's hypotheses concerning a biological basis for irrational thinking (perhaps through behaviour genetics research designs).
5 Test Ellis's hypothesis that global self-rating is almost always counter-productive, as there is little empirical evidence to support the view that *positive* global self-evaluation will ultimately prove self-defeating (such research would require the development of measurement procedures capable of distinguishing between unconditional self-acceptance and positive global self-rating).

In the area of therapy practice, Kendall et al. note the importance of conducting more rigorous studies on REBT's clinical efficacy.

With respect to designing and conducting such studies, they indicate the importance of ensuring that REBT is properly implemented, of using randomized clinical trials and of reporting the clinical significance of treatment outcomes. Kendall et al. also state the desirability of pursuing research that would help to elucidate mechanisms of change in REBT. Such studies, which are largely lacking in the REBT research literature, could examine issues such as whether improved self-acceptance in clients actually leads to improvements in psychological health. Finally, Kendall et al. note that there is no empirical evidence in support of the contention that rational-emotive psychoeducational programmes for well-adjusted children can help to prevent the development of future psychological disorders. Prior studies in this area have been limited insofar as they failed to conduct long-term post-treatment follow-up. It would, of course, be desirable to have some supporting data for the preventative utility of rational-emotive education programmes before recommending their widespread use in educational institutions.

As a result of his seemingly tireless efforts to promote and develop rational emotive behaviour therapy, it is likely that Albert Ellis will leave an enduring legacy with the fields of counselling and psychotherapy. While future generations of mental health practitioners may remember him first and foremost as a master therapist and theoretician, the broader implications of his work should also be remembered. Ellis has not merely invented a widely practised system of psychotherapy, he has created a philosophy of living which has the potential to help many human beings to lead happier, healthier and more productive lives.

Select Bibliography of Ellis's Works

Books

Reason and Emotion in Psychotherapy (1962). Secaucus, NJ: Lyle Stuart.

Humanistic Psychotherapy: The Rational-Emotive Approach (1973). New York: McGraw-Hill.

With R.A. Harper, *A New Guide to Rational Living* (1975). North Hollywood, CA: Wilshire Books.

With J.M. Whiteley (eds), *Theoretical and Empirical Foundations of Rational-Emotive Therapy* (1979). Monterey, CA: Brooks/Cole.

How to Maintain and Enhance your Rational-Emotive Therapy Gains (1984). New York: Institute for Rational-Emotive Therapy. (Pamphlet.)

Overcoming Resistance: Rational-Emotive Therapy with Difficult Clients (1985). New York: Springer.

With W. Dryden, *The Practice of Rational-Emotive Therapy* (1987). New York: Springer.

How to Stubbornly Refuse to Make Yourself Miserable about Anything – Yes, Anything! (1988). Secaucus, NJ: Lyle Stuart.

Chapters

'Research data supporting the clinical and personality hypotheses of RET and other cognitive-behavior therapies', in A. Ellis and R. Grieger (eds), *Handbook of Rational-Emotive Therapy* (1977). New York: Springer. pp. 35–71.

'The philosophic implications and dangers of some popular behavior therapy techniques', in M. Rosenbaum, C.M. Franks and Y. Jaffe (eds), *Perspectives on Behavior Therapy in the Eighties* (1983). New York: Springer. pp. 138–51.

'Failures in rational-emotive therapy', in E.B. Foa and P.M.G. Emmelkamp (eds), *Failures in Behavior Therapy* (1983). New York: Wiley. pp. 159–71.

'Dilemmas in giving warmth or love to clients (Interview)', in W. Dryden (ed.), *Therapists' Dilemmas* (1985). London: Harper & Row. pp. 5–16.

'On the origin and development of rational-emotive therapy', in W. Dryden (ed.), *Key Cases in Psychotherapy* (1987). London: Croom Helm. pp. 148–75.

'My life in clinical psychology', in C.E. Walker (ed.), *The History of Clinical Psychology in Autobiography* Vol. 1 (1991). Pacific Grove, CA: Brooks/Cole. pp. 1–37.

Articles

'The biological basis of human irrationality', *Journal of Individual Psychology*, 32 (1976): 145–68.

'Fun as psychotherapy', *Rational Living*, 12 (1) (1977): 2–6.

'Intimacy in psychotherapy', *Rational Living*, 12 (2) (1977): 13–19.

'Discomfort anxiety: a new cognitive-behavioral construct. Part 1', *Rational Living*, 14 (2) (1979): 3–8.

'The issue of force and energy in behavior change', *Journal of Contemporary Psychotherapy*, 10 (1979): 83–97.

'Discomfort anxiety: a new cognitive-behavioral construct. Part 2', *Rational Living*, 15 (1) (1980): 25–30.

'Rational-emotive therapy and cognitive-behavior therapy: similarities and differences', *Cognitive Therapy and Research*, 4 (4) (1980): 325–40.

'The value of efficiency in psychotherapy', *Psychotherapy: Theory, Research, and Practice*, 17 (4) (1980): 414–19.

'Must most psychotherapists remain as incompetent as they now are?', *Journal of Contemporary Psychotherapy*, 13 (1) (1982): 17–28.

'My philosophy of work and love', *Psychotherapy in Private Practice*, 1 (1) (1983): 43–9.

'How to deal with your most difficult client – you', *Psychotherapy in Private Practice*, 2 (1) (1984): 25–35.

'The impossibility of achieving consistently good mental health', *American Psychologist*, 42 (1987): 364–75.

'The revised ABC's of rational-emotive therapy (RET)', *Journal of Rational-Emotive and Cognitive-Behavior Therapy*, 9 (3) (1991): 139–72.

Related Works of Interest

Bernard, M.E. and DiGiuseppe, R. (eds) (1989) *Inside Rational-Emotive Therapy: A Critical Appraisal of the Theory and Therapy of Albert Ellis*. San Diego, CA: Academic Press.

Walen, S.R., DiGiuseppe, R. and Dryden, W. (1992) *A Practitioner's Guide to Rational-Emotive Therapy* (2nd edn). New York: Oxford University Press.

Wiener, D. (1988) *Albert Ellis: Passionate Skeptic*. New York: Praeger.

Yankura, J. and Dryden, W. (1990) *Doing RET: Albert Ellis in Action*. New York: Springer.

The following book contains an excellent selection of some of Ellis's most important papers:

Dryden, W. (ed.) (1990) *The Essential Albert Ellis: Seminal Writings on Psychotherapy*. New York: Springer.

References

Adler, A. (1927) *Understanding Human Nature.* New York: Greenberg.

Adler, A. (1929) *The Science of Living.* New York: Greenberg.

Allport, G.W. and Ross, J.M. (1967) 'Personal religious orientation and prejudice', *Journal of Personality and Social Psychology,* 5: 432–43.

Bandura, A. (1977) *Social Learning Theory.* Englewood Cliffs, NJ: Prentice-Hall.

Beck, A.T. (1963) 'Thinking and depression', *Archives of General Psychiatry,* 9: 324–33.

Beck, A.T. (1967) *Depression.* New York: Harper (Hoeber).

Beck, A.T. (1976) *Cognitive Therapy and the Emotional Disorders.* New York: International Universities Press.

Beck, A.T. and Emery, G. (1985) *Anxiety Disorders and Phobias: A Cognitive Perspective.* New York: Basic Books.

Beck, A.T., Freeman A. and associates (1990) *Cognitive Therapy of Personality Disorders.* New York: Guilford.

Beck, A.T., Rush, A., Shaw, B.F. and Emery, G. (1979) *Cognitive Therapy of Depression.* New York: Guilford.

Bergin, A.E. (1983) 'Religiosity and mental health: a critical re-evaluation and meta-analysis', *Professional Psychology: Theory, Research, and Practice,* 14: 170–84.

Bernard, M.E. (1986) *Staying Rational in an Irrational World: Albert Ellis and Rational-Emotive Therapy.* Carlton, Australia: McCulloch.

Bernard, M.E. and Joyce, M.R. (1984) *Rational-Emotive Therapy with Children and Adolescents.* New York: John Wiley & Sons.

Burns, D.D. (1980) *Feeling Good: The New Mood Therapy.* New York: Morrow.

Dames, J. and Ellis, A. (1991) 'Counseling in the classroom: interview with Albert Ellis', *Journal of Rational-Emotive and Cognitive-Behavior Therapy,* 9 (4): 247–63.

DiGiuseppe, R. (1991) 'Comprehensive cognitive disputing in rational-emotive therapy', in M. Bernard (ed.), *Using Rational-Emotive Therapy Effectively.* New York: Plenum.

DiGiuseppe, R.A., Robin, M.W. and Dryden, W. (1990) 'On the compatibility of rational-emotive therapy and Judeo-Christian philosophy: a focus on clinical strategies', *Journal of Cognitive Psychotherapy: An International Quarterly,* 4 (4): 355–68.

DiMattia, D. (1993) 'RET in the workplace', *Journal of Rational-Emotive and Cognitive-Behavior Therapy,* 11 (1): 3–5.

DiMattia, D. and Lega, L. (1990) *Will the Real Albert Ellis Please Stand Up?* New York: Institute for Rational-Emotive Therapy.

DiMattia, D. and Mennen, S. (1990) *Rational Effectiveness Training: Increasing Personal Productivity at Work.* New York: Institute for Rational-Emotive Therapy.

Dolliver, R.H. (1979) 'The relationship of rational-emotive therapy to other psychotherapies and personality theories', in A. Ellis and J.M. Whiteley (eds), *Theoretical and Empirical Foundations of Rational-Emotive Therapy*. Monterey, CA: Brooks/Cole. pp. 203–17.

Dryden, W. (1987a) *Counselling Individuals: The Rational-Emotive Approach*. London: Whurr.

Dryden, W. (1987b) 'Where is the evidence? Promoting quality RET research', in W. Dryden (ed.), *Current Issues in Rational-Emotive Therapy*. London: Croom Helm. pp. 192–201.

Dryden, W. (1990a) *Rational-Emotive Counselling in Action*. London: Sage.

Dryden, W. (ed.) (1990b) *The Essential Albert Ellis: Seminal Writings on Psychotherapy*. New York: Springer.

Dryden, W. and Backx, W. (1987) 'Problems in living: the Friday night workshop', in W. Dryden (ed.), *Current Issues in Rational-Emotive Therapy*. New York: Croom Helm. pp. 154–70.

Dryden, W. and Ellis, A. (1985) 'Dilemmas in giving warmth or love to clients (Interview)', in W. Dryden (ed.), *Therapists' Dilemmas*. London: Harper & Row. pp. 5–16.

Dryden, W. and Ellis, A. (1986) 'Rational-emotive therapy', in W. Dryden and W.L. Golden (eds), *Cognitive-Behavioural Approaches to Psychotherapy*. London: Harper & Row. pp. 129–68.

Dryden, W. and Ellis, A. (1987) 'Rational-emotive therapy: an update', in W. Dryden (ed.), *Current Issues in Rational-Emotive Therapy*. London: Croom Helm. pp. 1–45.

Dryden, W. and Ellis, A. (1988) 'Rational-emotive therapy', in K. Dobson (ed.), *Handbook of Cognitive-Behavioral Therapies*. New York, Guilford Press.

Dryden, W. and Ellis, A. (1989) 'Albert Ellis: an efficient and passionate life (Interview)', *Journal of Counseling and Development*, 67: 539–46.

Dryden, W., Ferguson, J. and Clark, T. (1989) 'Beliefs and inferences – a test of a rational-emotive hypothesis: 1. Performing in an academic seminar', *Journal of Rational-Emotive and Cognitive-Behavior Therapy*, 7 (3): 119–29.

Dryden, W., Ferguson, J. and Hylton, B. (1989) 'Beliefs and inferences – a test of a rational-emotive hypothesis: 3. On expectations about enjoying a party', *British Journal of Guidance and Counselling*, 17 (1): 68–75.

Dryden, W., Ferguson, J. and McTeague, S. (1989) 'Beliefs and inferences – a test of a rational-emotive hypothesis: 2. On the prospect of seeing a spider', *Psychological Reports*, 64: 115–23.

Dryden, W. and Gordon, J. (1990) *What is Rational-Emotive Therapy?* Loughton, Essex: Gale Centre Publications.

Dryden, W. and Yankura, J. (1993) *Counselling Individuals: A Rational-Emotive Handbook* (2nd edn). London: Whurr.

Dubois, P. (1907) *The Psychic Treatment of Nervous Disorders*. New York: Funk & Wagnalls.

Dyer, W. (1976) *Your Erroneous Zones*. New York: Funk & Wagnalls.

Ellis, A. (1946) 'The validity of personality questionnaires', *Psychological Bulletin*, 43: 385–440.

Ellis, A. (1947a) 'A comparison of the use of direct and indirect phrasing in personality questionnaires', *Psychological Monographs*, 61: iii–41.

Ellis, A. (1947b) 'Personality questionnaires', *Review of Educational Research*, 17: 101–9.

Ellis, A. (1948a) 'Questionnaire versus interview methods in the study of human love relationships. II. Uncategorized responses', *American Sociological Review*, 13: 62–5.

Ellis, A. (1948b) 'The relationship between personality inventory scores and other psychological test results', *Journal of Social Psychology*, 26: 287–9.

Ellis, A. (1949) 'Towards the improvement of psychoanalytic research', *Psychoanalytic Review*, 36: 123–43.

Ellis, A. (1950) *An Introduction to the Scientific Principles of Psychoanalysis*. Provincetown, MA: Journal Press.

Ellis, A. (1951) *The Folklore of Sex*. New York: Charles Boni. (Rev. edn, New York: Grove Press, 1961.)

Ellis, A. (1955a) 'New approaches to psychotherapy techniques', *Journal of Clinical Psychology Monograph Supplement*, 11: 1–53.

Ellis, A. (1955b) 'Psychotherapy techniques for use with psychotics', *American Journal of Psychotherapy*, 9: 452–76.

Ellis, A. (1956) 'An operational reformulation of some of the basic principles of psychoanalysis', *Psychoanalytic Review*, 43: 163–80.

Ellis, A. (1957a) 'Rational psychotherapy and individual psychology', *Journal of Individual Psychology*, 13 (1): 38–44.

Ellis, A. (1957b) *How to Live with a Neurotic: At Home and at Work*. New York: Crown (rev. edn, North Hollywood, CA: Wilshire Books, 1975.)

Ellis, A. (1957c) 'Outcome of employing three techniques of psychotherapy', *Journal of Clinical Psychology*, 13: 334–50.

Ellis, A. (1958) *Sex without Guilt*. New York: Lyle Stuart. (Rev. edn, 1965.)

Ellis, A. (1960) *The Art and Science of Love*. New York: Lyle Stuart.

Ellis, A. (1962) *Reason and Emotion in Psychotherapy*. Secaucus, NJ: Lyle Stuart.

Ellis, A. (1965a) *The Case for Sexual Liberty*. Tucson, AZ: Seymour Press.

Ellis, A. (1965b) 'Showing clients they are not worthless individuals', *Voices*, 1 (2): 74–7.

Ellis, A. (1967) 'Goals of psychotherapy', in A.R. Mahrer (ed.), *The Goals of Psychotherapy*. New York: Meredith. pp. 206–20.

Ellis, A. (1968) *Biographical Information Form*. New York: Institute for Rational-Emotive Therapy.

Ellis, A. (1969) *Suggested Procedures for a Weekend of Rational Encounter*. New York: Institute for Rational-Emotive Therapy.

Ellis, A. (1971) *Growth through Reason*. North Hollywood, CA: Wilshire Books.

Ellis, A. (1972a) 'Psychotherapy without tears', in A. Burton (ed.), *Twelve Therapists: How They Live and Actualize Themselves*. London: Jossey-Bass. pp. 103–26.

Ellis, A. (1972b) 'Helping people to get better rather than merely feel better', *Rational Living*, 7 (2): 2–9.

Ellis, A. (1973a) *Humanistic Psychotherapy: The Rational-Emotive Approach*. New York: McGraw-Hill.

Ellis, A. (1973b) 'My philosophy of psychotherapy', *Journal of Contemporary Psychotherapy*, 6 (1): 13–18. (Reprinted, New York: Institute for Rational-Emotive Therapy.)

Ellis, A. (1974) 'Cognitive aspects of abreactive therapy', *Voices*, 10 (1): 48–56.

Ellis, A. (1975) *RET Abolishes Most of the Human Ego* (pamphlet). New York: Institute for Rational-Emotive Therapy.

156   *Albert Ellis*

Ellis, A. (1976a) 'The biological basis of human irrationality', *Journal of Individual Psychology*, 32: 145–68.

Ellis, A. (1976b) *Sex and the Liberated Man*. Secaucus, NJ: Lyle Stuart.

Ellis, A. (1977a) 'Fun as psychotherapy', *Rational Living*, 12 (1): 2–6.

Ellis, A. (1977b) 'The basic clinical theory of rational-emotive therapy', in A. Ellis and R. Grieger (eds), *Handbook of Rational-Emotive Therapy*. New York: Springer. pp. 3–34.

Ellis, A. (1977c) 'Psychotherapy and the value of a human being', in A. Ellis and R. Grieger (eds), *Handbook of Rational-Emotive Therapy*. New York: Springer. pp. 99–112.

Ellis, A. (1977d) 'The rational-emotive facilitation of psychotherapeutic goals', in A. Ellis and R. Grieger (eds), *Handbook of Rational-Emotive Therapy*. New York: Springer. pp. 189–97.

Ellis, A. (1977e) 'Intimacy in psychotherapy', *Rational Living*, 12 (2): 13–19.

Ellis, A. (1977f) 'Research data supporting the clinical and personality hypotheses of RET and other cognitive-behavior therapies', in A. Ellis and R. Grieger (eds), *Handbook of Rational-Emotive Therapy*. New York: Springer. pp. 35–71.

Ellis, A. (1977g) *Anger: How to Live With and Without It*. Secaucus, NJ: Citadel Press.

Ellis, A. (1977h) 'A rational approach to interpretation', in A. Ellis and R. Grieger (eds), *Handbook of Rational-Emotive Therapy*. New York: Springer. pp. 216–24.

Ellis, A. (1978) 'Personality characteristics of rational-emotive therapists and other kinds of therapists', *Psychotherapy: Theory, Research and Practice*. 15: 329–32.

Ellis, A. (1979a) 'The biological basis of human irrationality: a reply to McBurnett and LaPointe', *Individual Psychology*, 35 (1): 111–16.

Ellis, A. (1979b) 'Discomfort anxiety: a new cognitive-behavioral construct. Part 1', *Rational Living*, 14 (2): 3–8.

Ellis, A. (1979c) 'The theory of rational-emotive therapy', in A. Ellis and J.M. Whiteley (eds), *Theoretical and Empirical Foundations of Rational-Emotive Therapy*. Monterey, CA: Brooks/Cole. pp. 33–60.

Ellis, A. (1979d) 'The issue of force and energy in behavior change', *Journal of Contemporary Psychotherapy*, 10: 83–97.

Ellis, A. (1979e) 'The practice of rational-emotive therapy', in A. Ellis and J.M. Whiteley (eds), *Theoretical and Empirical Foundations of Rational-Emotive Therapy*. Monterey, CA: Brooks/Cole. pp. 61-100.

Ellis, A. (1979f) 'Rejoinder: elegant and inelegant RET', in A. Ellis and J.M. Whiteley (eds), *Theoretical and Empirical Foundations of Rational-Emotive Therapy*. Monterey, CA: Brooks/Cole. pp. 240–67.

Ellis, A. (1979g) 'Toward a new theory of personality', in A. Ellis and J.M. Whiteley (eds), *Theoretical and Empirical Foundations of Rational-Emotive Therapy*. Monterey, CA: Brooks/Cole. pp. 7–32.

Ellis, A. (1980a) 'Discomfort anxiety: a new cognitive-behavioral construct. Part 2', *Rational Living*, 15 (1): 25–30.

Ellis, A. (1980b) 'The value of efficiency in psychotherapy', *Psychotherapy: Theory, Research, and Practice*, 17 (4): 414–19.

Ellis, A. (1980c) 'Rational-emotive therapy and cognitive behavior therapy: similarities and differences', *Cognitive Therapy and Research*, 4 (4): 325–40.

Ellis, A. (1982) 'Must most psychotherapists remain as incompetent as they now are?', *Journal of Contemporary Psychotherapy*, 13 (1): 17–28.

Ellis, A. (1983a) 'The philosophic implications and dangers of some popular behavior therapy techniques', in M. Rosenbaum, C.M. Franks and Y. Jaffe (eds), *Perspective on Behavior Therapy in the Eighties*. New York: Springer. pp. 138–51.

Ellis, A. (1983b) 'Rational-emotive therapy (RET) approaches to overcoming resistance. 1: Common forms of resistance', *British Journal of Cognitive Psychotherapy*, 1 (1): 28–38.

Ellis, A. (1983c) 'Rational-emotive therapy (RET) approaches to overcoming resistance. 2: How RET disputes clients' irrational resistance-creating beliefs', *British Journal of Cognitive Psychotherapy*, 1 (2): 1–16.

Ellis, A. (1983d) 'Failures in rational-emotive therapy', in E.B. Foa and P.M.G. Emmelkamp (eds), *Failures in Behavior Therapy*. New York: Wiley. pp. 159–71.

Ellis, A. (1983e) 'My philosophy of work and love', *Psychotherapy in Private Practice*, 1 (1): 43–9.

Ellis, A. (1983f) *The Case against Religiosity*. New York: Institute for Rational-Emotive Therapy.

Ellis, A. (1984a) 'Rational-emotive therapy (RET) approaches to overcoming resistance. 3: Using emotive and behavioral techniques of overcoming resistance', *British Journal of Cognitive Psychotherapy*, 2 (1): 11–26.

Ellis, A. (1984b) 'How to deal with your most difficult client – you', *Psychotherapy in Private Practice*, 2 (1): 25–35.

Ellis, A. (1984c) *How to Maintain and Enhance your Rational-Emotive Therapy Gains*. New York: Institute for Rational-Emotive Therapy.

Ellis, A. (1984d) 'Foreword: Cognitive, affective, and behavioural aspects of rational-emotive therapy', in W. Dryden, *Rational-Emotive Therapy: Fundamentals and Innovations*. London: Croom Helm. pp. vii–xxvi.

Ellis, A. (1984e) 'The place of meditation in cognitive-behavior therapy and rational-emotive therapy', in D.H. Shapiro Jr and R.N. Walsh (eds), *Meditation: Classic and Contemporary Perspectives*. New York: Aldine. pp. 671–3.

Ellis, A. (1984f) 'Is the unified interaction approach to cognitive-behavior modification a reinvention of the wheel?' *Clinical Psychology Review*, 4: 215–18.

Ellis, A. (1985a) 'Why Alcoholics Anonymous is probably doing more harm than good by its insistence on a Higher Power' (Review of *Alcoholics Anonymous*, 3rd Edn). *Employee Assistance Quarterly*, 1 (1): 95–7.

Ellis, A. (1985b) 'Approaches to overcoming resistance. 4: Handling special kinds of clients', *British Journal of Cognitive Psychotherapy*, 3 (1): 26–42.

Ellis, A. (1985c) *Overcoming Resistance: Rational-Emotive Therapy with Difficult Clients*. New York: Springer.

Ellis, A. (1986a) 'Thoughts on supervising counselors and therapists', *Association for Counselor Education and Supervision Newsletter*, Summer: 3–5.

Ellis, A. (1986b) 'Do some religious beliefs help create emotional disturbance?' *Psychotherapy in Private Practice*, 4 (4): 101–6.

Ellis, A. (1987a) 'The impossibility of achieving consistently good mental health', *American Psychologist*, 42: 364–75.

Ellis, A. (1987b) 'On the origin and development of rational-emotive therapy', in W. Dryden (ed.), *Key Cases in Psychotherapy*. London: Croom Helm. pp. 148–75.

Ellis, A. (1987c) 'The evolution of rational-emotive therapy (RET) and cognitive-behavior therapy (CBT)', in J.K. Zeig (ed.), *The Evolution of Psychotherapy*. New York: Brunner/Mazel. pp. 107–33.

Ellis, A. (1987d) 'The use of rational humorous songs in psychotherapy', in W.F. Fry Jr and W.A. Salameh (eds), *Handbook of Humor in Psychotherapy: Advances in the Clinical Use of Humor.* Sarasota, FL: Professional Resource Exchange, Inc.

Ellis, A. (1988a) 'Psychotherapies that promote profound philosophical change foster behavioral change', *Journal of Integrative and Eclectic Psychotherapy,* 7 (4): 397–402.

Ellis, A. (1988b) *How to Stubbornly Refuse to Make Yourself Miserable about Anything – Yes, Anything!* Secaucus, NJ: Lyle Stuart.

Ellis, A. (1988c) 'Are there "rationalist" and "constructivist" camps of the cognitive therapies? A response to Michael Mahoney', *The Cognitive Behaviorist,* 10: 13–16.

Ellis, A. (1989a) 'The history of cognition in psychotherapy', in A. Freeman. K.M. Simon, L.E. Beutler and H. Aronowitz (eds), *Comprehensive Handbook of Cognitive Therapy.* New York: Plenum. pp. 5–19.

Ellis, A. (1989b) 'The courage to change', in P.L. Berman (ed.), *The Courage to Grow Old.* New York: Ballantine. pp. 131–6.

Ellis, A. (1989c) 'Comments on my critics', in M.E. Bernard and R. DiGiuseppe (eds), *Inside Rational-Emotive Therapy: A Critical Appraisal of the Theory and Therapy of Albert Ellis.* San Diego, CA: Academic Press. pp. 199–233.

Ellis, A. (1990a) 'Intimacy in rational-emotive therapy', in W. Dryden (ed.), *The Essential Albert Ellis: Seminal Writings on Psychotherapy.* New York: Springer. pp. 184–201.

Ellis, A. (1990b) 'Rational-emotive therapy approaches to overcoming resistance', in W. Dryden (ed.), *The Essential Albert Ellis: Seminal Writings on Psychotherapy.* New York: Springer. pp. 265–99.

Ellis, A. (1990c) 'Is rational-emotive therapy (RET) "rationalist" or "constructivist"?' in W. Dryden (ed.), *The Essential Albert Ellis: Seminal Writings on Psychotherapy.* New York: Springer. pp. 114–41.

Ellis, A. (1991a) 'My life in clinical psychology', in C.E. Walker (ed.), *The History of Clinical Psychology in Autobiography,* Vol. 1. Pacific Grove, CA: Brooks/Cole. pp. 1–37.

Ellis, A. (1991b) 'The revised ABC's of rational-emotive therapy (RET)', *Journal of Rational-Emotive and Cognitive-Behavior Therapy,* 9 (3): 139–72.

Ellis, A. (1991c) 'Using RET effectively: reflections and interview', in M.E. Bernard (ed.), *Using Rational-Emotive Therapy Effectively.* New York: Plenum. pp. 1–33.

Ellis, A. (1991d) 'Achieving self-actualization', in A. Jones and R. Crandall (eds), *Handbook of Self-actualization,* Special Issue of *Journal of Social Behavior and Personality,* 6 (5): 1–18.

Ellis, A. (1992) 'My current views on rational-emotive therapy (RET) and religiousness', *Journal of Rational-Emotive and Cognitive-Behavior Therapy.* 10 (1): 37–40.

Ellis, A. (1993) 'Constructivism and rational-emotive therapy: a critique of Richard Wessler's critique', *Psychotherapy,* 30: 531–2.

Ellis, A., Abrams, M. and Dengelegi, L. (1992) *The Art and Science of Rational Eating.* Fort Lee, NJ: Barricade Books.

Ellis, A. and Becker, I. (1982) *A Guide to Personal Happiness.* North Hollywood, CA: Wilshire.

Ellis, A. and Bernard, M.E. (eds) (1983) *Rational-Emotive Approaches to the Problems of Childhood.* New York: Plenum.

Ellis, A. and Bernard, M.E. (1985) 'What is rational-emotive therapy (RET)?' in A. Ellis and R.M. Grieger (eds), *Handbook of Rational-Emotive Therapy* Vol. 2. New York: Springer. pp. 3–30.

Ellis, A. and Brancale, R. (1956) *The Psychology of Sex Offenders*. Springfield, IL: Charles C. Thomas.

Ellis, A. and Dryden, W. (1987) *The Practice of Rational-Emotive Therapy*. New York: Springer.

Ellis, A. and Dryden, W. (1990) 'The basic practice of RET', in W. Dryden (ed.), *The Essential Albert Ellis: Seminal Writings on Psychotherapy*. New York: Springer. pp. 145–83.

Ellis, A. and Grieger, R. (1977) 'The present and the future of RET', in A. Ellis and R. Grieger (eds), *Handbook of Rational-Emotive Therapy*. New York: Springer. pp. 421–33.

Ellis, A. and Harper, R.A. (1961) *A Guide to Successful Marriage*. North Hollywood, CA: Wilshire Books.

Ellis, A. and Harper, R.A. (1975) *A New Guide to Rational Living*. North Hollywood, CA: Wilshire Books.

Ellis, A. and Hunter, P. (1991) *Why Am I Always Broke? (How to be Sane about Money)*. Secaucus, NJ: Lyle Stuart.

Ellis, A. and Knaus, W. (1977) *Overcoming Procrastination*. New York: Institute for Rational-Emotive Therapy.

Ellis, A., McInerney, J., DiGiuseppe, R. and Yeager, R. (1988) *RET with Alcoholics and Substance Abusers*. New York: Pergamon.

Ellis, A., Sichel, J., Yeager, R., DiMattia, D, and DiGiuseppe, R. (1989) *Rational-Emotive Couples Therapy*. New York: Pergamon.

Ellis, A. and Velten, E. (1992) *When AA doesn't Work for You: Rational Steps to Quitting Alcohol*. Fort Lee, NJ: Barricade Books.

Ellis, A. and Whiteley, J.M. (1979) *Theoretical and Empirical Foundations of Rational-Emotive Therapy*. Monterey, CA: Brooks/Cole.

Ellis, A. and Yeager, R.J. (1989) *Why Some Therapies Don't Work*. New York: Prometheus.

Eschenroeder, C. (1982) 'How rational is rational-emotive therapy? A critical appraisal of its theoretical foundations and therapeutic methods', *Cognitive Therapy and Research*, 6: 381–92.

Ferenczi, S. (1952) *Further Contributions to the Theory and Technique of Psychoanalysis*. New York: Basic Books.

Goldfried, M.R. and Davison, G. (1976) *Clinical Behavior Therapy*. New York: Holt, Rinehart & Winston.

Grieger, R.M. and Boyd, I. (1980) *Rational-Emotive Therapy: A Skills Based Approach*. New York: Van Nostrand-Reinhold.

Guidano, V.F. (1988) 'A systems, process-oriented approach to cognitive therapy', in K.S. Dobson (ed.), *Handbook of Cognitive-Behavioral Therapies*. New York: Guilford. pp. 307–56.

Guidano, V.F. and Liotti, G. (1983) *Cognitive Processes and Emotional Disorders*. New York: Guilford.

Haaga, D.A.F. and Davison, G.C. (1989) 'Outcome studies of rational-emotive therapy', in M.E. Bernard and R. DiGiuseppe (eds), *Inside Rational-Emotive Therapy: A Critical Appraisal of the Theory and Therapy of Albert Ellis*. San Diego, CA: Academic Press. pp. 155–97.

Heesacker, M., Heppner, P.P. and Rogers, M.E. (1982) 'Classics and emerging classics in counseling psychology', *Journal of Counseling Psychology*, 29: 400–5.

Hoellen, B. and Ellis, A. (1986) 'An interview with Albert Ellis', *Psychotherapy in Private Practice*, 4 (2): 81–98.

Horney, K. (1950) *Neurosis and Human Growth*. New York: Norton.

Huber, C. and Baruth, L. (1989) *Rational-Emotive Family Therapy: A Systems Perspective*. New York: Springer.

Johnson, W.B. (1992) 'Rational-emotive therapy and religiousness: a review', *Journal of Rational-Emotive and Cognitive-Behavior Therapy*, 10 (1): 21–35.

Jones, M.C. (1924) 'A laboratory study of fear: the case of Peter', *Journal of Genetic Psychology*, 31: 308–15.

Joyce-Moniz, L. (1985) 'Epistemological theory and constructivism', in M.J. Mahoney and A. Freeman (eds), *Cognition and Psychotherapy*. New York: Plenum. pp. 143–80.

Kanfer, F.H. and Goldstein, A.P. (eds), (1975) *Helping People Change*. New York: Pergamon.

Kelly, G. (1955) *The Psychology of Personal Constructs*. New York: Norton.

Kendall, P.C., Haaga, D.A.F., Ellis, A., Bernard, M., DiGiuseppe, R. and Kassinove, H. (submitted for publication) 'Rational-Emotive Therapy in the 1990's and Beyond: Current Status, Recent Revisions, and Research Questions.'

Kendall, P.C. and Hollon, S.D. (eds) (1979) *Cognitive Behavioral Interventions: Theory, Research, and Procedures*. New York: Academic Press.

King, R.R. (1978) 'Evangelical Christians and professional counseling: a conflict of values?' *Journal of Psychology and Theology*. 6: 276–81.

Knaus, W. (1974) *Rational-Emotive Education: A Manual for Elementary School Teachers*. New York: Institute for Rational Living.

Lange, A. and Jakubowski, P. (1976) *Responsible Assertive Behavior*. Champaign, IL: Research Press.

Lazarus, A.A. (1971) *Behavior Therapy and Beyond*. New York: McGraw-Hill.

Lazarus, A.A. (1976) *Multimodal Therapy*. New York: Springer.

Lazarus, A.A. (1979) 'Can RET become a cult?', in A. Ellis and J.M. Whiteley (eds), *Theoretical and Empirical Foundations of Rational-Emotive Therapy*. Monterey, CA: Brooks/Cole. pp. 236–39.

Lazarus, A.A. (1989) 'The practice of rational-emotive therapy', in M.E. Bernard and R. DiGiuseppe (eds), *Inside Rational-Emotive Therapy: A Critical Appraisal of the Theory and Therapy of Albert Ellis*. San Diego, CA: Academic Press. pp. 95–112.

Lazarus, A.A. and Fay, A. (1975) *I Can If I Want To*. New York: Morrow.

Mahoney, M.J. (1974) *Cognition and Behavior Modification*. Cambridge, MA: Ballinger.

Mahoney, M.J. (1976) *Scientist as Subject*. Cambridge, MA: Ballinger.

Mahoney, M.J. (1979) 'A critical analysis of rational-emotive theory and therapy', in A. Ellis and J.M. Whiteley (eds), *Theoretical and Empirical Foundations of Rational-Emotive Therapy*. Monterey, CA: Brooks/Cole. pp. 177–80.

Mahoney, M.J. (1988) 'The cognitive sciences and psychotherapy: patterns in a developing relationship', in K.S. Dobson (ed.), *Handbook of the Cognitive-Behavioral Therapies*. New York: Guilford. pp. 357–86.

Mahoney, M.J. and Gabriel, T.J. (1987) 'Psychotherapy and cognitive sciences: an evolving alliance', *Journal of Cognitive Psychotherapy*, 1: 39–59.

Mahoney, M.J., Lyddon, W.J. and Alford, D.J. (1989) 'An evaluation of the rational-emotive theory of psychotherapy', in M.E. Bernard and R. DiGiuseppe (eds),

Inside Rational-Emotive Therapy: A Critical Appraisal of the Theory and Therapy of Albert Ellis. San Diego, CA: Academic Press. pp. 69–94.

Maultsby Jr, M.C. and Ellis A. (1974) *Technique for Using Rational-Emotive Imagery*. New York: Institute for Rational-Emotive Therapy.

McBurnett, K. and LaPointe, K.A. (1978) 'Concerning a biological basis of human irrationality', *Journal of Individual Psychology*, 34: 201–5.

McMinn, M.R. and Lebold, C.J. (1989) 'Collaborative efforts in cognitive therapy with religious clients', *Journal of Psychology and Theology*, 17: 101–9.

Meichenbaum, D. (1977) *Cognitive-Behavior Modification*. New York: Plenum.

Meichenbaum, D. (1979) 'Dr. Ellis, please stand up', in A. Ellis and J.M. Whiteley (eds), *Theoretical and Empirical Foundations of Rational-Emotive Therapy*. Monterey, CA: Brooks/Cole. pp. 174–6.

Pepper, S.C. (1942) *World Hypotheses*. Berkeley: University of California Press.

Raimy, V. (1975) *Misunderstandings of the Self*. San Francisco: Jossey-Bass.

Rational Effectiveness Training Systems (1987) *Mind over Myths: Managing Difficult Situations in the Workplace* (cassette recordings). New York: Institute for Rational-Emotive Therapy.

Ruth, W.J. (1992) 'Irrational thinking in humans: an evolutionary proposal for Ellis' genetic postulate', *Journal of Rational-Emotive and Cognitive-Behavior Therapy*, 10 (1): 3–20.

Salter, A. (1949) *Conditioned Reflex Therapy*. New York: Creative Age.

Saltzman, N. and Ellis, A. (1986) 'Clinical exchange', *International Journal of Eclectic Psychotherapy*, 5 (3): 276–8.

Schwartz, R.M. (1982) 'Cognitive-behavior modification: a conceptual review', *Clinical Psychology Review*, 2: 267–93.

Schwartz, R.M. (1984) 'Is rational-emotive therapy a truly unified interactive approach? A reply to Ellis', *Clinical Psychology Review*, 4: 219–26.

Sharkey, P.W. and Maloney, H.N. (1986) 'Religiosity and emotional disturbance: a test of Ellis's thesis in his own counseling center', *Psychotherapy: Theory, Research, and Practice*, 23: 640–1.

Sichel, J. and Ellis, A. (1984) *Self-help Report Form*. New York: Institute for Rational-Emotive Therapy.

Smith, D. (1982) 'Trends in counseling and psychotherapy', *American Psychologist*, 37: 802–9.

Spivack, G. and Shure, M. (1974) *Social Adjustment in Young Children*. San Francisco: Jossey-Bass.

Stark, R. (1971) 'Psychopathology and religious commitment', *Review of Religious Research*. 12: 165–76.

Trimpey, J. (1992) *Rational Recovery from Alcoholism: The Small Book*. New York: Delacorte Press.

Vernon, A. (1989a) *Thinking, Feeling, Behaving: An Emotional Education Curriculum for Children Grades 1–6*. Champaign, IL: Research Press.

Vernon, A. (1989b) *Thinking, Feeling, Behaving: An Emotional Education Curriculum for Children Grades 7–12*. Champaign, IL: Research Press.

Walen, S.R., DiGiuseppe, R. and Dryden, W. (1992) *A Practitioner's Guide to Rational-Emotive Therapy*, 2nd edn. New York: Oxford University Press.

Warren, R. and McLellarn, R.W. (1987) 'What do RET therapists think they are doing? an international survey', *Journal of Rational-Emotive Therapy*, 5: 71–91.

Warren, R., McLellarn, R.W. and Ellis, A. (1987) 'Albert Ellis' personal responses to the survey of rational-emotive therapists', *Journal of Rational-Emotive Therapy*, 5 (2): 92–107.

Warren, R. and Zgourides, G. (1991) *Anxiety Disorders: A Rational-Emotive Perspective*. New York: Pergamon.

Watson, J.B. and Rayner, R. (1920) 'Conditioned emotional reactions', *Journal of Experimental Psychology*, 3: 1–14.

Weinrach, S. and Ellis, A. (1980) 'Unconventional therapist: Albert Ellis (Interview)', *Personnel and Guidance Journal*, 59: 152–60.

Wessler, R.L. (1992) 'Constructivism and rational-emotive therapy: a critique', *Psychotherapy*, 29 (4): 620–5.

Wiener, D. (1988) *Albert Ellis: Passionate Skeptic*. New York: Praeger.

Winegar, N. (1992) *The Clinician's Guide to Managed Mental Health Care*. Binghamton, NY: Haworth Press.

Wolpe, J. (1958). *Psychotherapy by Reciprocal Inhibition*. Stanford, CA: Stanford University Press.

Wolpe, J. (1983) *The Practice of Behavior Therapy*, 3rd edn. New York: Pergamon.

Woolfolk, R.L. and Sass, L.A. (1989) 'Philosophical foundations of rational-emotive therapy', in M.E. Bernard and R. DiGiuseppe (eds), *Inside Rational-Emotive Therapy: A Critical Appraisal of the Theory and Therapy of Albert Ellis*. San Diego, CA: Academic Press. pp. 9–26.

Yankura, J. and Dryden, W. (1990) *Doing RET: Albert Ellis in Action*. New York: Springer.

Young, H. (1989) 'Practising RET with Bible-belt Christians', in W. Dryden (ed.), *Howard Young: Rational Therapist*. Loughton, Essex: Gale Centre Publications. pp. 77–96.

Ziegler, D.J. (1989) 'A critique of the rational-emotive theory of personality', in M.E. Bernard and R. DiGiuseppe (eds), *Inside Rational-Emotive Therapy: A Critical Appraisal of the Theory and Therapy of Albert Ellis*. San Diego, CA: Academic Press. pp. 27–45.

Index